The Expert Witness

R. H. Mildred
F.R.I.C.S., F.C.I.Arb., F.F.B

Past Chairman of the Chartered
Institute of Arbitrators

with a foreword by
The Right Honourable Lord Diplock

George Godwin
London and New York

George Godwin
Longman House
Burnt Mill, Harlow, Essex, UK

A division of Longman Group Ltd, London

*Published in the United States of America
by Longman Inc., New York*

First published 1982

British Library Cataloguing in Publication Data

Mildred, R H
   The expert witness.
   1. Evidence, Expert – Great Britain
   I. Title
   344.107'67   KD7521
   ISBN 0-7114-56801-1

Typeset by Oxford Verbatim Limited.
Printed in Great Britain by William Clowes (Beccles) Ltd.
Beccles and London.

To my wife,
lovingly and in gratitude
for her patience

Contents

Contents

Foreword

R. H. Mildred was a distinguished Chairman of the Chartered Institute of Arbitrators as well as a distinguished expert in construction work. So he has great experience both at the giving end and the receiving end of expert evidence. This has enabled him to write a practical handbook which should be a great help to anyone who may find himself required to give evidence as an expert witness before a court or other tribunal or in an arbitration. My own experience of expert evidence has been limited to consulting with expert witnesses and examining and cross-examining them in my role as counsel and listening to and evaluating their evidence in my subsequent role as judge; but in both those roles I too would have benefited from having read this book if only Mr. Mildred had found time to write it three decades ago. Perhaps I ought also to confess to authorship of the Law Reform Committee's Report on Evidence of Opinion and Expert Evidence of October 1970 from which Mr. Mildred quotes and which led to the passing of the Civil Evidence Act, 1972. I do so for the purpose of stressing once again how much in a wide variety of cases the judiciary rely upon the candour and expertise of expert witnesses to enable justice to be done. In the very first chapter of this book, attention is drawn to the function of the expert witness as being to assist the tribunal to come to a true and proper decision. Honesty in expression of his opinion on matters within the field of his expertise is a characteristic of experts with professional qualifications that I have always, and happily with justification, been able to take for granted; but order and clarity of exposition and ability to explain technical matters in terms adapted to the kind of tribunal before whom the evidence is given, which may be entirely uninstructed in that particular subject or may share in whole or part the expert witness's own expertise, these are not gifts with which experts are endowed by nature. Like the expertise itself, they need to be learnt. Here at last is a practical handbook admirably adapted for that purpose. I commend it warmly to all those who may be called upon to give expert evidence that will best assist the tribunal to come to a true and proper decision upon matters which involve the subject of their expertise.

DIPLOCK

Introduction

The purpose of this book is to give practical assistance to those who may be called upon to give evidence as experts. The term 'expert witness' can be a misnomer, conveying the idea that the witness is an expert at giving evidence rather than an expert in a particular field of knowledge. Nevertheless, one who is expert in his chosen profession may not, for lack of training or for other reasons, be able to prepare and present evidence competently when called upon to do so. My own experience of arbitration proceedings over a period of years has convinced me that this is so. Much so-called expert evidence that I have heard could only be described as bad.

This book then, while making no claim at all to being a legal textbook, does set out to explain the basic principles underlying the giving of expert evidence and to show how such evidence should properly be given.

While much of it has been written with the construction industry in mind it is hoped that it may be found helpful to those in other spheres of activity and that they can relate their own expertise to what is written here.

My thanks are due primarily to colleagues in the Chartered Institute of Arbitrators not only for the idea of this book but also for assistance in its preparation.

The late Mr William James, CBE, FRICS, a past President of the Institute, was for long in the forefront of those urging the necessity of training in the giving of expert evidence. In his inaugural address in 1970 he urged the taking of 'a greater interest in the training of expert witnesses who are a vital part of arbitration procedure – for example by lectures on the principles and practice of the preparation of proofs of evidence . . . and perhaps in drafting a code of conduct for them much on the lines which govern barristers, and solicitors as officers of the court'. Mr James was speaking as the head of a body primarily concerned with arbitration, but what he then said applies to evidence given before tribunals of all kinds. Under his tireless guidance the Chartered Institute of Arbitrators has set up syllabuses and courses for training in the giving of expert evidence and has prepared guide-lines of good practice for expert witnesses.

I am also particularly indebted to Mr G. J. R. Hickmott, Past Chairman of the Chartered Institute of Arbitrators, and to Mr F. E. Rehder, CVO, a Vice-President, for their help, and to my son, Mr Paul Mildred, for much valuable advice. I am also grateful to Miss McOlvin and to Mrs Harris for the typing and retyping of proofs.

The term 'tribunal' has been used throughout the book to include all those courts and tribunals before which expert evidence may have to be given. A brief outline of the judicial system is given in the Appendix. The laws, specific rules and detailed procedures described in this book are applicable only to England and Wales and are not necessarily applicable to Scotland and Northern Ireland. Readers practising in those countries will be aware of the differences in these matters that apply locally. The extracts from the Rules of the Supreme Court and from the Lands Tribunal Rules are taken from the 1980 rules in each case.

My examples are based upon actual cases and experiences, but I have changed details – mainly names, places and dates – to avoid any possible embarrassment.

Finally, I am most grateful to Lord Diplock, a past President of the Chartered Institute of Arbitrators, for the interest he has shown in the writing of this book, for his patience in reading the proofs and for the honour he has done me in writing the foreword.

Acknowledgement

My thanks are due to those who have given permission to reproduce material in this book:

To the Controller, Her Majesty's Stationery Office, for the Civil Evidence Acts 1968 and 1972 and extracts from the Rules of the Supreme Court and from the Lands Tribunal Rules (Crown Copyright); for extracts from the Law Reform Committee Seventeenth Report (Evidence of Opinion and Expert Evidence October 1970 Cmnd 4489) (referred to in the text as 'The Law Reform Committee Report') and for extracts from 'The Complete Plain Words' (Sir Ernest Gowers, revised by Sir Bruce Fraser).

To the Institution of Civil Engineers for extracts from a paper by the Rt. Hon. Lord Macmillan of Aberfeldy PC, GCVO, LLD, HON MICE entitled 'The Giving of Evidence' read before the Institution on 20 June 1946.

To the Chartered Institute of Arbitrators for quotations from papers read before the Institute by Lord Roskill and Lord Justice Donaldson.

To Sweet & Maxwell Limited for extracts from Phipson's Manual of the Law of Evidence (see Chapter 3, Definitions); and for extracts from Osborne's Concise Law Dictionary (Sixth Edition) (see Appendix A, Glossary of Legal Terms).

To Macdonald & Evans Limited for extracts from General Principles of English Law by P. W. D. Redmond, (Fifth Edition, revised by J. P. Price and I. N. Stevens) (See Appendix B, Types of Tribunal.)

Chapter 1 The Function of the Expert Witness

THE PURPOSE OF TRIBUNALS

The function of a tribunal is to decide the matter or matters in issue. For this purpose it has material put before it which should enable the tribunal to come to a true and proper decision. This material is called evidence, and evidence is put before the tribunal by witnesses. The purpose of witnesses is therefore to assist the tribunal to come to a true and proper decision.

This may sound trite and obvious, but it is a fundamental fact that must be understood from the outset: the sole true purpose of a witness whether lay or expert – and the difference between the two will be explained later – is to assist the tribunal. The fact that a witness is called and in certain circumstances may be paid by one side or the other does not alter the position.

WITNESSES

Broadly speaking, witnesses are of two kinds, witnesses of fact (lay witnesses) and witnesses of opinion (expert witnesses).

A witness of fact has personal knowledge of events which happened in the past and were perceived by his physical senses. Thus a witness of fact in a case involving a motor accident may give evidence as to place, time, the vehicles involved and the facts relating to the occurrence generally. Such a witness is not normally permitted to express an opinion arising from his knowledge of those facts, e.g. he would not give his opinion as to the cause of the accident or the liability of the parties in relation to it.

This rule is however becoming increasingly eroded because statements about speed and distance made by such a witness are expressions of opinion deriving from his experience in such matters applied to the facts which he perceived at the time of the accident which he is describing.

A witness of opinion has special knowledge acquired for example in the course of professional training and experience. This knowledge enables the witness to assist the tribunal in coming to a decision by giving his opinion on the facts before the tribunal. Thus in the case of the motor accident referred to above, an expert witness who was not at the scene of the accident when it occurred could give an opinion based on examination of the vehicles involved as to whether the accident was caused by a mechanical failure or not.

Two quotations from legal authorities describe the role of the expert witness. The first is from Best's treatise on Evidence and runs as follows:

> 'On questions of science, skill, trade and the like, persons conversant with the subject-matter . . . are permitted to give their opinions in evidence; i.e. to state conclusions whether drawn from facts which have fallen under their own observation or from such as are proved at the trial by other evidence. Thus, medical practitioners are allowed to give their opinions as to the probable cause of disease or death or the probable result of a wound or injury; artists to give their opinions as to the genuineness of a picture; shipbuilders to give their opinions as to the seaworthiness of a ship; and the like.'

The other passage is from Smith's 'Leading Cases':

> 'The opinion of witnesses possessing peculiar skill is admissible whenever the subject-matter of inquiry is such that inexperienced persons are unlikely to prove capable of forming a correct judgement upon it without such assistance; in other words, when it so far partakes of the nature of a science or art as to require a course of previous habit or study in order to the attainment of a knowledge of it.'*

---

* Lord Macmillan of Aberfeldy 'The Giving of Evidence'.

The Law Reform Committee Report sets out the difference between evidence of fact and evidence of opinion. The reader should acquaint himself with the Report and in particular with those sections reproduced in the Appendix. Paragraph 29 headed 'The Nature of Experts' Reports', while leading on to the question of the disclosure of reports, sums up a judicial view of the expert witness, as follows:

'All expert opinion is based upon facts which the expert, for the purposes of his opinion, assumes to be true. However highly qualified the expert, if the facts which he has assumed differ in any material respect from those which are ultimately accepted by the judge at the trial as being the true facts, the opinion of the expert is not directed to the real issue upon which his expert assistance is needed to enable justice to be done. This consideration points to a relevant distinction between experts' reports made before trial, according to the kinds of facts upon which the opinion of the expert is based. If they are facts of a kind which, so far as they are not already agreed, can be ascertained before the trial with reasonable certainty by the expert himself by the exercise of his own powers of observation, or are within the general professional knowledge or experience, a report made by him before the trial is likely to be directed to the actual issue upon which his assistance is needed. We should regard as being within an expert's general professional knowledge or experience any matters which are within the common knowledge of the profession by reason of their having been published in books or professional journals or which have been observed by the expert himself in the course of his professional studies or practice. If, on the other hand, the report is based upon facts which are in dispute between the parties to the action, the expert's opinion given before trial upon a version of the facts supplied by the party on whose behalf he is instructed will only be of assistance if that version is ultimately accepted as the true version by the judge at the trial. Furthermore, experts' reports in the latter category involve disclosing alleged facts which the party instructing the expert will seek to prove at the trial by witnesses other than the expert himself and to this extent involve disclosing material which will be included in the proofs of those witnesses. If the opinion of the expert based upon the alleged facts so disclosed is unfavourable to another party to the action, there might be a temptation to that other party to trim the version of the facts presented by him and his witnesses at the trial so as to weaken or destroy the factual basis of the unfavourable expert opinion. We would not wish to overstress this risk. Most witnesses of fact, even though they are parties to litigation, are honest and intend to be candid. But human memory is fallible and parties in particular are prone to convince themselves without any intentional dishonesty that what would most assist their own case was what actually happened.'

An arbitrator being a person appointed with special expertise in the subject matter of the dipute may not need the assistance of expert witnesses but a lay tribunal will need guidance on technical matters.

A witness of opinion may also be a witness of fact. An example of this is the engineer engaged on construction works and present at the time of a failure of those works, such as the collapse of a retaining wall. His evidence of fact would relate to the actual events as witnessed by him and perceived with his own physical senses. His evidence as an expert would be his opinion based on the known facts as to the cause of the collapse.

In such a position his duty as a witness on oath is to give his true opinion based upon his knowledge and experience and not to act as an advocate for the party calling him. His prime function is to assist the tribunal by giving a fair and honest opinion and not to assist his client to win his case, despite his being called and paid by the client.

There is therefore a clear distinction between that of the expert and that of the advocate, although in certain types of procedure the expert may have to fulfil those two roles. While the prime function of an advocate (be he counsel, solicitor or lay advocate) is to assist the tribunal to a just decision, his duty is to persuade the court as to the construction it should place upon the facts and the opinions placed before it. His own opinion on the merits or otherwise of his client's case are of no concern to the tribunal. Normally the advocate accepts any brief sent to him unless there is a strong reason for his not doing so, and only in the most exceptional circumstances does an advocate give evidence himself. The opinion of an advocate on the merits or demerits of the case he is arguing is irrelevant and not to be stated by him. He can 'submit' a proposition without alleging, averring or denying it.

The opinion of an expert can be of great importance to the tribunal in giving guidance on technical matters on which the court could not be expected to be informed and it is therefore essential that the witness of opinion should speak only the truth as he sees it regardless as to whether his opinion on a certain aspect of his evidence supports his client's case or not. If an expert cannot in honesty support his client's case in principle he should not accept instructions in the matter. Truth, not sophistry, is the business of the expert.

Many matters touched on above will be dealt with more fully later in this book but it is necessary that the true function of the expert witness be fully understood at the outset.

ASSESSORS

In certain types of case, notably in the Admiralty Division of the High Court, an expert assessor sits with the judge. His function is not to give evidence but, (in an Admiralty action):

'to provide the judge with such general information as will enable him to take judicial notice of facts which are notorious to those experienced in seamanship about the corresponding characteristics of ships and of traffic conditions upon navigable waters, so that he may be qualified to reach an informed opinion about the standards of care to be observed by reasonable users of those waters. In effect, the nautical assessor's function is to enlarge the field of matters of which the judge may take judicial notice so as to include matters of navigation and general seamanship.

Consultation between the judge and the nautical assessor is continual and informal, both in court and in the judge's room. The advice which the judge receives from the assessor is not normally disclosed to counsel during the course of the hearing, although the judge may do so if he thinks fit. In his judgment he does usually state what advice he has received on particular matters and whether he has accepted it or not. But he is under no obligation to do so and the practice is not uniform among all judges.'*

As the assessor does not give evidence his opinions cannot be subjected to the test of cross-examination.

---

* Law Reform Committee Report paras 9 to 10.

COURT EXPERTS

Provision for the appointment of a court expert is made by Order 40 of the Rules of the Supreme Court (See Appendix) but this power is rarely used, except in cases involving the custody or care of infants.

Chapter 2   The Qualifications and Duties of the Expert

BASIC QUALIFICATIONS OF A PERSON ACTING AS AN EXPERT

The basic qualifications required of a person called to act as an expert are briefly these:

1. Relevant professional qualifications and experience in the field of the dispute. A lack of professional qualifications will not debar a person from appearing as an expert nor will it render his evidence inadmissible but it may count against him on the score of weight of evidence as compared with that of a witness who has appropriate professional qualifications.

2. A general knowledge of the law of evidence; of the principles of damages; of professional negligence and breach of contractual duty and of practice in relation to the duties of expert witnesses during the proceedings.

3. The ability to express himself both orally and in writing in clear, simple language that can readily be understood by a lay tribunal.

4. The ability to weigh facts and to draw logical conclusions from them.

5. The ability to view a problem impartially.

The expert must constantly strive to keep himself informed of developments in all fields affecting his own professional expertise including legislation, codes of practice, standard forms of contract, codes of conduct and so on. This can be done by such means as technical journals, the reading and hearing of learned papers and contact with professional colleagues within one's own discipline. It is paradoxical but nevertheless true that a person with the longest experience in a particular expertise may not be as well informed as a person who has not been engaged in that speciality for so long but who has taken greater pains to keep his knowledge up-to-date.

THE DUTY OF THE EXPERT

The duty of the expert is to assist the tribunal. His evidence must be truthful. He is not required to volunteer information beyond that required of him. He should be prepared to enlarge his answer to a question put to him if he considers that his reply – properly made to the question as framed – does not give a true picture.

An expert is not permitted to give his interpretation of the law; that is a matter for the tribunal. An expert is immune from subsequent proceedings arising out of his opinions expressed in evidence as to the matters in issue, whether or not these opinions take the form of criticism of other parties involved in the proceedings, and provided always that it cannot be shown that he has perjured himself or has been a party to our attempted fraud arising out of the proceedings. The principle was confirmed by Lord Salmon in the case of *Sutcliffe* v. *Thackrah and Others* [1974] AC 727 when he said, 'It is well settled that judges, barristers, solicitors, jurors and witnesses enjoy an absolute immunity from any form of civil action being brought against them in respect of anything they say or do in Court during the course of a trial'.

THE EXPERT'S DUTY OF SKILL AND CARE

A person holding himself out as possessing a special skill or skills owes a duty of care arising from the carrying on of those skills. Liability consequent upon failure to take due care may arise in tort and in contract.

For a plaintiff to succeed in an action for negligence he must prove:-

1. that the defendant owed him a duty of care;
2. that there was a breach of that duty;
3. that as a result the plaintiff has suffered damage.

The following quotations from *Donoghue* v *Stevenson* [1932] AC 562 (HL) illustrate the question of duty of care. 'You must take reasonable care to avoid acts or omissions which you can reasonably foresee would be likely to injure your neighbour. Who, then, is my neighbour? The answer seems to be – persons who are so closely affected by my act that I ought reasonably to have them in contemplation as being so affected when I am directing my mind to the acts or omissions which are called in question.'

The standard of care is that of the ordinary prudent man holding himself out as possessing a particular skill; such a person must demonstrate a standard of skill commonly found in such persons. 'A defendant charged with negligence can clear himself if he shows that he acted in accord with general and approved practice' (*Marshall* v *Lindsey County Council* [1935] 1 KB 516, 540 (CA)).

Lord Denning MR in *Greaves & Co (Contractors) Ltd* v *Baynham Meikle and Partners* [1975] 3 All ER 104 said 'It seems to me that in the ordinary employment of a professional man, whether it is a medical man, a lawyer, or an accountant, an architect or an engineer, his duty is to use reasonable care and skill in the course of his employment. The extent of this duty was described by McNair J in *Bolam* v *Friern Hospital Management Committee,* approved by the Privy Council in *Chin Keow* v *Government of Malaysia*:

'. . . where you get a situation which involves the use of some special skill or competence, then the test whether there has been negligence or not is not the test of the man on the top of a Clapham omnibus, because he has not got this special skill. The test is the standard of the ordinary skilled man exercising and professing to have that special skill . . . It is well-established law that it is sufficient if he exercises the ordinary skill of an ordinary competent man exercising that particular art.'

In applying that test, it may be remembered that the measures to be taken by a professional man depend on the circumstances of the case.'

A case in the Canadian Court of Appeal further illustrates this point. The owner of a building site asked a professional engineer for a copy of a soils report which he had made at the request of the architect. The report was based on examination of shallow test holes on the site. Although the engineer told the architect that a deep soil test was necessary he signed a letter to the owner describing his examination of the test holes and stating his opinion of the load bearing capacity of the soil without indicating that the examination was inadequate as a basis for judging that capacity. It was held that he was under a duty of care to the owner to inform him of the inadequacy of the test. *Surrey (District)* v *Carroll-Hatch & Associates Ltd* [1979] 101 DLR (3d) 218 (Court of Appeal of British Columbia). *Hedley Byrne & Co Ltd* v *Heller & Partners Ltd* [1964] AC 465, HL, applied.

A person claiming an especially high degree of skill in a particular field will owe a correspondingly higher duty of care.

Breach of the duty of care lies in failure to exercise the requisite skill. Should an expert make a statement carelessly and the plaintiff in acting upon it suffer damage in consequence, the plaintiff will have an action for damages unless a valid disclaimer had been made by the defendant at the time of making the statement.

In the leading case of *Hedley Byrne* v *Heller* [1964] AC 465 the decision of the House of Lords was that a person making an innocent but negligent misstatement resulting in financial loss is liable, even if there is no contractual relationship between the person making the statement and the party to whom it is made. The fact that the statement is inaccurate or false is not enough to establish liability: it must also be proved that the statement was made carelessly or negligently. Lord Denning MR in *Esso Petroleum Co Ltd* v *Mardon* [1976] 2 All ER 15 said:

> 'A professional man may give advice under a contract for reward; or without a contract, in pursuance of a voluntary assumption of responsibility, gratuitously without reward. In either case he is under one and the same duty to use reasonable care: see *Cassidy* v *Ministry of Health*. In the one case it is by reason of a term implied by law. In the other, it is by reason of a duty imposed by law. For a breach of that duty he is liable in damages; and those damages should be, and are, the same, whether he is sued in contract or in tort.'*

In the case of *Sutcliffe* v *Thackrah and Others* referred to above, the House of Lords held that the building owner who suffered loss as a result of the negligent issue of certificates by the architect was entitled in law to recover that loss from the architect.

* See also *Mutual Life Assurance* v *Evatt* [1971] AC 793; [1971] 1 All ER 150 *Arenson* v *Casson* [1977] AC 405; [1975] 3 All ER 901.

Chapter 3   Evidence

The subject of evidence is a highly technical one and an outline only of the main points is attempted in this book. For a full exposition of the subject reference must be made to one of the standard works.

In England, trials follow the adversarial system, that is to say, the parties themselves decide what evidence shall be placed before the tribunal, which adjudicates only on the matters put before it. In the inquisitorial system, usual on the continent, the court conducts the enquiry with the assistance of the parties.

DEFINITIONS

(Taken from 'Phipson's Manual of Evidence'.) See also Glossary of Legal Terms in the Appendix.

Proof

Proof is the method by which the existence or non-existence of some fact may be established to the satisfaction of the tribunal charged with the duty of trying fact. In civil proceedings (normally tried without a jury) the tribunal may decide on the balance of probabilities. In criminal proceedings conviction should only be made when the jury are satisfied that they are sure of the guilt of the accused beyond any reasonable doubt. The general rule on burden of proof is that he who asserts must prove (whether the allegation be an affirmative one or a negative one) and not he who denies. If the tribunal is not satisifed on the balance of probabilities that the assertion is correct then judgment must be given for the other party.

Evidence

Evidence may be defined as the testimony of witnesses and the production of documents and things which may be used for the purpose of proof in legal proceedings.

Admissibility

A fact is admissible if the law allows it to be proved by evidence. To be admissible a fact must be either in issue or have some degree of relevance to the facts in issue. Evidence is admissible if the rules of law allow it to be adduced before the tribunal.

Relevance

Relevance is the relationship between one fact and another wherein, according to the rules of logic and the common experience of men, the existence of one renders probable the existence or non-existence of the other. All admissible facts are relevant, but not all relevant facts are admissible.

Best and inferior evidence

The rule, which is called the best evidence rule, rejected inferior evidence such as a copy of a document, or a witness's description of an object, if the original was obtainable. It was also thought to make original rather than hearsay evidence necessary. The rule has greatly declined in importance in civil matters, and now mainly applies in the proof of private documents, where the terms generally used are 'primary' and 'secondary' rather than 'best' and 'inferior'.

Direct and circumstantial evidence

Direct evidence consists either of the testimony of the witness who perceived the fact, or the production of the document which constitutes the fact, e.g. the lease of a farm, or of the thing which is in question. A witness who says that he saw the accident in respect of which damages are being claimed in the action, or that he was present with the other witness and saw the testator sign his will and with the other witness attested that will, is giving direct evidence; circum-stantial evidence is evidence which, although not directly establishing the existence or non-existence of the fact required to be proved, is admissible in order to enable the tribunal to decide whether that fact did or did not exist.

Original and hearsay evidence

The term 'original evidence' as distinguished from 'hearsay' is used to indicate the evidence of a witness who deposes to facts of his own knowledge. If his information is derived from other persons, and he himself has no personal knowledge of the facts to which he deposes, then his evidence is said to be hearsay.

Real evidence

This consists primarily of the inspection of objects, other than docu-ments, produced for examination by the tribunal of fact; non-portable objects and places may be viewed out of court by the tribunal of fact. The real evidence of a view is as much evidence as the testimony of witnesses, and, provided that the matter is not a technical one where the assistance of expert witnesses is required, the tribunal is entitled to prefer the impression gained from a view to the testimony of witnesses.

Discovery of documents

In actions begun by writ, lists of documents must be served by each party after close of pleadings, and any party entitled to have discovery may serve a notice requiring an affidavit verifying the list of docu-ments. Also, in any action, however begun, the court may order any party to make and serve a list of documents, and may order him to make a verifying affidavit.

Facts in issue

These are those facts which a plaintiff must prove in order to establish his claim and those facts which the defendant must prove in order to establish a defence set up by him, but only when the fact alleged by the one party is not admitted by the other party. Facts which are admitted, expressly or by implication, are not in issue. Facts in issue are, there-

fore, determinable primarily by the substantive law, and secondly by
the pleadings.

Facts relevant to the issue

These are facts which render probable the existence or non-existence
of a fact in issue, or some other relevant fact. Facts relevant to the issue
are in the main determined by ordinary logic and experience.

Privilege

Communications and documents passing between a client and his legal
adviser in professional confidence are privileged. Communications
between the legal adviser and a third party in contemplation of litigation are also privileged.

'Without Prejudice' statements

An admission made in the course of negotiations as a genuine attempt
to compromise or to settle a dispute cannot be given in evidence
without the consent of the party who made the statement. The addition of the phrase 'without prejudice' to a document does not of itself
make that document inadmissible, nor does its absence necessarily
make it admissible.

THE DIFFICULTY OF OBTAINING
ACCURATE TESTIMONY OF FACT

Lord Macmillan of Aberfeldy in his paper on 'The Giving of Evidence'
has this to say on the subject of accurate testimony:

'No one who has had to deal with problems of fact can have failed to
be struck by the extraordinary difficulty of obtaining accurate testimony. A distinguished Professor of Psychology in one of the
American universities published, in 1923, a book entitled Psychology
and the Day's Work. He was anxious to ascertain what really were
the limits of human fallibility in the matter of evidence, and he
devised an interesting laboratory experiment.
   He had an intelligent class of young men and women of the usual

14

age. The class consisted of some twenty-nine students. He arranged one day, without the knowledge of his class, that an incident should happen in his class-room. He planned that three members of the class and another student – two men and two women, all well known to the class – should wait outside in the corridor; that in the middle of his lecture, quite unexpectedly, they should burst into the room; that one of them should drop a brick – I do not mean a metaphorical brick – and that each of the others should do something else; each had allotted to him one definite thing to do. It was an incident of the simplest possible character, without any of the complications of an ordinary accident in the street, where people's powers of observation are limited and the situation is complicated. He staged the simplest possible series of operations.

The door was burst open, and these four people came in. The class was very much upset, but the professor at once calmed them, saying, 'This is a pure experiment. In the last thirty seconds' – the whole incident lasted thirty seconds – 'something has happened in your presence in this room. I want you to take your note-books and write down what has happened in this room in these last thirty seconds.'

Everything was favourable to the ascertainment and recording of truth. Nobody had a motive to find anybody guilty of anything. The transaction to be recorded was free from all complications, and all had been within the direct vision of the witnesses. Each of them wrote down in his note-book what he had seen, and the papers were collected and collated by the professor.

The most extraordinary results were found. There was hardly one of those observers, who had no motive to distort the truth and every opportunity to observe the facts, who did not make a mistake. As a matter of fact, there was not one accurate record of what had happened. Only three knew that four people had come into the room. One said that a pistol had been fired. No pistol had been fired, but one of the intruders had flourished a banana and detonated a percussion cap. A woman student said that one of women who came in was wearing a red hat. She was not, but she had on other occasions worn a red hat. That was a case of what psychologists call transferred memory, and so on. The whole thing was typical of the kind of errors that arise. This experiment has been to me a very grave warning of the fallibility of human testimony on a matter of fact.

In giving evidence on fact, therefore, it is exceedingly important that one should be most critical of oneself. It is easy to reconstruct a

15

scene as one would wish it to have been or as one thought it was, rather than as it actually was. When, therefore, you are concerned with a question of giving evidence about a matter of fact, it is of the utmost importance that you should be most scrupulously accurate and not say anything about which you are not quite clear. Verify your facts so far as the means are still available to you for verification and see that you have got everything as accurate as you possibly can. Where you feel uncertainty, candidly confess it.'

While the quotation above refers to the difficulty of obtaining accurate testimony of fact, parallel conclusions can be drawn in the matter of evidence of opinion, namely the necessity of accurate observation and recording, and of thoroughness in all aspects of preparation for the giving of expert evidence.

THE CIVIL EVIDENCE ACTS

The Civil Evidence Act 1968 (See Appendix)

Under this Act hearsay evidence of fact became admissible by virtue of the provisions of the Act. Any form of hearsay can be admitted in civil proceedings by agreement of the parties. Out-of-court statements are admissible as evidence of facts stated (Sec. 2). Sec. 4 deals with the admissibility of records and Sec. 5 with the admissibility of statements produced by computers. Sec. 9 deals with the admissibility of certain hearsay evidence formerly admissible at common law. Sec. 10 gives certain definitions of terms used and deals with application to arbitrations and to references under the County Courts Act 1959.

The Civil Evidence Act 1972 (See Appendix)

This Act deals with the admissibility in evidence of hearsay statements of opinion and in particular the reception of expert evidence, including provisions as to the disclosure of expert's reports. It also applies to arbitration proceedings.

Chapter 4   Instructions

INSTRUCTIONS GENERALLY

Receipt of instructions may come about in a variety of ways, namely:

1. As a result of present and/or previous engagement in the subject matter of the dispute e.g. as resident engineer on a civil engineering contract, or as site architect on a large building contract.
2. As a result of recommendation by one of the parties to the dispute, or by a fellow professional.
3. By reputation as an expert in the particular field.
4. By recommendation from a professional society. Many societies maintain lists of practitioners capable of taking on this class of work.

In the first case given above his interest in the matter will be known to the parties. In the other cases he will not have detailed knowledge of the dispute, but if he has an interest in or connection with the party wishing to have him appear for them he must make this clear at the outset to instructing solicitors so that they can decide whether or not he should be asked to act. An example of such an interest could be as a shareholder of the firm involved, or of one of its subsidiaries; an example of connection could be as having acted professionally in the past for the firm involved.

Before professional societies put forward names on application from one or the other parties in a particular matter they normally make enquiries of the persons they approach so that any interest or connection will be made known before a name is put forward.

FURTHER MATTERS BEFORE ACCEPTANCE OF INSTRUCTIONS

When the twin hurdles of interest and connection have been satisfactorily cleared, there are further matters to be considered by the potential witness before he can accept instructions.

First, he must make himself sufficiently acquainted with those aspects of the dispute upon which he will be called to act to be sure that it falls within the scope of his personal knowledge and experience. A person should never accept instructions on the basis of a mere general description of the dispute or of his likely duties. To do so could well result in a person finding himself asked to act beyond his proper scope with consequent failure to give proper advice or, worse, finding himself in the position of having to withdraw after acceptance of instructions and the doing of a certain amount of work. In either case the outcome could be disastrous for the client firm.

Second, having acquainted himself sufficiently with the dispute he must make up his mind as to whether his opinion will assist the client or not. Frank advice even at this preliminary stage could well be of greater value to the client than much detailed and costly work later on.

In this connection the expert should be aware of the possible pitfall of making a preliminary site visit accompanied by the client and/or his legal and other professional advisers. On such an occasion he is likely to be assailed with such hair-raising accounts of the enormity of the behaviour of the opposing party or of its failure to execute work to the standard laid down, that the expert may find it difficult to form a dispassionate view of the matter, but it is essential that he should do so.

Third, he must consider carefully whether he can act within the required time scale, having regard to all his other commitments. This is of great importance as it is not unknown for experts to be approached at far too late a stage in the proceedings, when adequate time for the work involved is unlikely to be given, and detailed reports being called for within days of a matter coming to trial. If no mention is made of time scale in the original enquiry, then the question must be raised by the person being approached.

These matters will need careful thought, despite the person concerned being urged for a quick answer because of pressure of time on the party's other advisors.

If a merely factual report is required, involving evidence of fact as distinct from evidence of opinion, instructions may be accepted more readily because certain of the considerations referred to above will not apply with such force.

ACCEPTANCE OF INSTRUCTIONS

Having decided that he can properly act in the matter the expert should then ask for instructions in writing, on receipt of which he should give his acceptance, also in writing. In his letter of acceptance he should state his charges: these are normally in terms of hourly rates although there may be cases where a lump sum fee is appropriate. Solicitors commonly ask to be given some idea of the overall fee involved, though this is rarely an easy question to answer.

In cases involving legal aid, authority is needed for the instruction of an expert. Such authority is usually given for the solicitor to incur fees up to a stated limit.

The letter of acceptance should also deal with such matters as travelling and hotel expenses, secretarial charges, charges for laboratory and similar tests, and whether the fee will be subject to Value Added Tax or not. An expert's bill of costs may in certain cases be taxed by the Taxing Master, an official of the court whose function it is to deal with costs according to the scales ordered by the judgment. In these circumstances it is wise for the expert to seek the advice of his instructing solicitor when drawing up his bill of costs. If, however, the expert's terms are clearly set out and he calls for, and obtains, a written acceptance of them by his client, this forms a contract under which fees are payable irrespective of any taxation reduction by the Court.

An expert should not under any circumstances agree to charge his fee on a 'payment by results' system. Such an arrangement could only undermine his approach to the matter and destroy the whole basis of his appearing as an independent witness of opinion. In the same way an expert should not accept an instruction to give evidence in support of his client's case. This would be held in cross-examination to bias his judgment and prejudice his impartiality. In such cases the expert should get his instruction altered before he accepts, so that he can give his evidence honestly and impartially.

Chapter 5 Preparation of the Case: Preliminary procedure

Normally the first duty of the expert on acceptance of instructions is to acquaint himself as quickly as possible with all matters relevant to the questions with which he has to deal. A useful outline of the matter can often be obtained by a preliminary meeting with the instructing solicitor who will explain the salient points of the case. This must be followed by a complete examination of all the relevant documents. In construction cases these could comprise:- contract agreement and conditions; contract drawings and drawings issued during the progress of the work; specification; bills of quantities; architects' instructions and certificates; final account; files of correspondence; lists of defects, and so on. Comparable sets of documents would be required for cases involving other branches of expertise.

Documents prepared by counsel whether in the form of advice, opinion or pleadings may be in existence at this stage, either in draft or in settled form, and they should be carefully studied, especially as they may set out further information required by counsel.

This examination of documents is an absolutely essential preliminary step in many types of case, although if carried out thoroughly it can be an arduous process. Two immediate matters may result from it. The first is a request for further documents if it is clear that some are missing. The second is a further meeting with instructing solicitors for the pupose of clarifying and/or amending instructions and this may in turn involve the redrafting of pleadings. If the expert considers that his instructions are perhaps too narrowly drawn, or that they miss points of detail which he thinks should be dealt with, or that they need amendment in other ways, he should get this done in agreement with instructing solicitors at the earliest possible moment to avoid difficulties later on.

Another important matter at this stage is for the expert to get in touch with other experts appearing on the same side. This is done through instructing solicitors. The purpose of this is to gain knowledge of their approach to the problems with which they have to deal and, where there is any likelihood of overlapping of evidence, to decide who is to deal with points that may be considered to fall within the purview of more than one expert. Tribunals generally are averse to repetitious evidence by experts; not only is this wasteful of time and expensive, but it may also have the effect of confusing the issues rather than clarifying them.

A further and perhaps more important aspect is that if overlapping of evidence does occur, opposing counsel will make every effort in cross-examination to show that the experts are contradicting each other. It is therefore vital that areas of evidence be defined beforehand. In this way a witness can make it clear when under cross-examination that he has not considered matters forming part of the expert evidence of a witness on the same side and that therefore he cannot deal with the points raised by counsel.

REPORTS

Following the matters set out above, the next duty of the expert is normally the production of a report. According to circumstances, this may be prepared after pleadings have been drafted or settled, in which case it will be directed to matters set out in those pleadings, or it may be prepared at a much earlier stage of the proceedings and may form the basis for parts of the pleadings.

Again, there are differences between reports prepared on instructions when litigation or advice on a matter in contention is in contemplation and those prepared for the purpose of exchange between the parties. Reports in the former category are privileged documents and may be used by a legal adviser to decide whether or not to proceed in a certain matter, and if so, how. Section 2(3) of the Civil Evidence Act 1972 makes provision under the rules of court for enabling the court in any civil proceedings to direct the exchange of experts' reports before they can be produced as evidence.

DRAFTING OF REPORT

The format of a report will depend on which of the two classes referred to above it falls into, and the following headings may therefore be regarded as no more than a general guide.

1. History of instructions, and terms of reference.
2. List of documents examined.
3. Inspection of subject matter of dispute, whether by site visit or other means.
4. Facts noted from inspection.
5. Conclusions drawn.

In certain cases inspection may not be of assistance or even possible and the conclusions will in those circumstances have to be based on the available documents. Typical examples are disputes arising from a completed demolition contract or from the sinking of a ship in deep water.

INSPECTION

The inspection is a matter of great importance, forming as it does in most cases one of the most important bases of a report. The instructions given to the expert, as well as the documents he has studied, may have enabled him to make a list of matters to be dealt with at the inspection. This will be of great assistance not only as a time-saver but also in ensuring as far as possible that items are not overlooked. There is nothing more annoying than to have to make a lengthy second journey merely to note an item that could easily have been dealt with at the first visit. It is often advisable to make a further visit when the report is in draft to ensure that it is complete in every respect and also to give an opportunity for second thoughts on the conclusions drawn. This may not always be possible as directions may have been given by the Court restricting the number of visits.

Certain other points in connection with the note-taking of the site visit should be mentioned, as follows:

1. Date and time of visit.

2. Other persons present.
3. Weather, if relevant to the report.
4. Photographs can be of material assistance in a report. Particular care must be taken to note exactly what is represented on the photographs, so that they can be proved at the hearing.
5. Note-taking should be as full as possible so that all matters come to mind later. A periodical note of the time at certain stages of the inspection can be of assistance in this.
6. It may be that a Scott schedule (see Chapter 8) has already been prepared. If so, the schedule must be worked through item by item so that nothing is missed.
7. In certain types of case it may be necessary for such things as samples of materials, or mechanical parts to be taken for laboratory testing. This will be done by agreement with the other side through instructing solicitors. Full particulars of date, substance, quantity taken, etc must be recorded both in notes and in the label attached to the sample or article. Notes and label should then be signed on behalf of both parties.

FURTHER POINTS ON THE DRAFTING OF A REPORT

At this stage it is necessary to examine the case very closely from the point of view of the other side; to consider the lines of argument that they will put forward and how best they may be countered. It is particularly important to recognise and pinpoint the weaknesses in one's own case so that all concerned, especially instructing solicitors and counsel, are aware of them and are forewarned. No case is completely watertight and there are bound to be some weaknesses somewhere. It is up to the expert to bring these out as early as possible so that they do not become an embarrassment at the hearing. This can easily happen if a witness is faced in cross-examination by questions directed to an aspect of the case that he had failed to identify and to deal with. In addition such an event can only hinder counsel's presentation of the case.

As an example from the construction industry, an expert may be called in support of a contractor's claim for direct loss and expense arising from delays in completion. The usual heads of claim such as the incidence of variations ordered by the architect and the failure of the architect to provide information at the appropriate time will have been advanced, but the expert must apprise himself of counter-arguments e.g. changes in managerial staff causing dislocation at site; shortages of labour and materials; time taken remedying defective work; delays caused by sub-contractors stopping work because of failure by the contractor to pay them, and so on. These must be gone into and if possible evaluated in the expert's report. Thus the advocate will be aware of them and may well decide to take the sting out of the arguments (or at any rate mitigate their effect) by dealing with them in examination-in-chief rather than leave it to opposing counsel to raise in cross-examination.

This leads on to the trap of the 'cast-iron case'. By this is meant the case which appears to be so obviously sound that one cannot at first sight imagine any defence to it. This is the type of case that needs the utmost care when considering it from the opponent's point of view because unless the likely lines of defence are uncovered and means to rebut them put forward, it is practically certain that they will come as an unpleasant surprise to the unwary witness when he is under cross-examination. It is too late to say to oneself 'If only I had thought of that' when being subjected to a relentless and totally unexpected line of questioning.

To sum up, the keynote at this stage in the preparation of a case – as indeed at every stage – is thoroughness, thoroughness in general approach coupled with thoroughness in matters of detail. Such thoroughness breeds confidence, and confidence can be conveyed to the tribunal by the manner of the expert's evidence.

THE NATIVE TONGUE

The use of plain, clear English is as necessary in the drafting of a written report as it is in giving oral evidence. Too often reports are a mass of verbiage which defeat their whole object by failing to convey the intended meaning to the reader. Long-windedness breeds ambiguity. Often, too, the use of technical jargon in place of simple, direct terms tends merely to confuse. In general, short words are preferable to long ones. Masters of the written word show their skill over the whole range of the language, but nowhere more so than in their use of short, simple words.

The Expert Witness

The following rules taken from 'The Complete Plain Words' put the matter in a nutshell.

'Use no more words than are necessary to express your meaning, for if you use more you are likely to obscure it and to tire your reader. In particular do not use superfluous adjectives and adverbs and do not use roundabout phrases where single words would serve.

Use familiar words rather than the far-fetched, if they express your meaning equally well; for the familiar are more likely to be readily understood.

Use words with a precise meaning rather than those that are vague, for they will obviously serve better to make your meaning clear; and in particular prefer concrete words to abstract, for they are more likely to have a precise meaning.'

Chapter 6 Preparation of the Case: Action after submitting a report

After the expert has submitted his report and it has been considered by instructing solicitors and by the advocate who will present the case he will in all probability be called into conference with the lawyers acting in the matter. The purpose of such conferences will be to elicit further information from the expert in order to clarify points that may be obscure or not adequately dealt with, to discuss the line that the other side may take in regard to the expert's evidence or the case generally, and to decide the tactics of presenting the case generally. Such conferences, particularly when conducted by counsel, can be prolonged and exhausting affairs. Counsel are accustomed to work long hours at a high degree of concentration and they expect other people to do the same. It is therefore essential for the expert to have all his facts – and his papers – ready and to be prepared to work long and irregular hours with counsel.

In these circumstances it is particularly important for the expert to recall and maintain at all times his independent, impartial approach. However persuasive counsel may be, and in however many different ways a point may be put to him, the expert must refuse to amend his report to suit the advocate's lines of attack unless he can in all honesty do so. Failure to maintain his stance in conference may later on lead to his downfall in cross-examination.

Equally important is the need to take the opportunity of a conference to emphasise directly to counsel the weak points of one's own case. This will not only assist counsel in deciding whether such points should be brought out in examination-in-chief or be left for cross-examination by the other side. If these points go to the whole root of the case, emphasis at an early stage may lead to a settlement beneficial, in view of the saving in costs, to both parties.

AGREEMENT OF 'FIGURES AS FIGURES'

At these preliminary stages the expert may be instructed to agree facts and figures with his opposite number appearing for the other side. This is an important way of narrowing the field of conflict and so enabling the tribunal to reach a conclusion more easily and quickly. The approach to the opposing side will normally be made through instructing solicitors and the expert should not under any circumstances make such an approach without having first received express instructions to do so. In addition he must restrict himself to those matters on which he has been given authority to deal and none other.

The matters to be dealt with in this way may be questions both of ascertainable fact and of professional judgment. For example, in a construction dispute, the ascertainable facts may be the dimensions and constructional characteristics of a building, the materials of which the various parts are built. On the other hand they may be the rates of wages payable to workpeople at certain dates under national wage agreements. Questions involving professional judgment could involve the cost of making good defective work (regardless of the reason as to why the work was defective) or of completing work left unfinished (again, regardless as to why it was left incomplete in the first place).

In other types of cases involving acquisition of land or property a schedule of condition as agreed by experts acting for the two parties is essential. Again, facts regarding the position and description of a property may be agreed. Such an agreement can be embodied in a plan or other document forming part of an agreed bundle.

The basis of the facts to be agreed must be established at the outset otherwise confusion may be worse compounded. For instance, if floor areas of a building are to be agreed, it must be decided whether or not internal walls and partitions are to be taken into account, to say nothing of circulating areas such as staircases and corridors. It is singularly unhelpful to a tribunal to be given two widely differing figures for the floor area of a building merely because the experts failed to agree on the basis for calculating the areas.

When agreement has been reached by the experts on the matters on which they were instructed the agreed documents should be endorsed with appropriate wording, e.g. 'These facts and figures are agreed as facts and figures entirely without prejudice in regard to liability on the matters in dispute between the parties', and the endorsement signed by both parties.

Occasions may arise where agreement can be reached on certain of the figures in a document but not on others. An example of this would be priced bills of quantities produced by both sides. The actual quantities of work as measured in the bills could be agreed by the experts (and the documents endorsed to that effect) while disagreement remained on the rates to be applied to the various items of measured work. It is helpful in respect of any of the points that are disagreed to state why they disagree with the opposing opinion.

PROOF OF EVIDENCE

At this stage in the proceedings the expert may be called upon to produce a proof of evidence.

A proof of evidence differs from a report in that the former is prepared for the information of the advocate who will call him. The proof takes the form of a written statement of what the witness will say, covering all his intended evidence. It will deal with the facts (which the witness may have elicited himself or which may have been available to him in other ways) and the conclusions which he has deduced from those facts. If the expert has had the opportunity of examining the reports of opposing witnesses his proof should also state where he differs from them and his grounds for doing so. His conclusions should not be mere statements but should be supported by his reasoning.

The proof should start with the words: 'Mr John Brown (giving the witness's name) will say'. It should therefore be written in the first person, giving force to the personal nature of the evidence.

The proof should start with the identification of the witness (name and address) and then go on to set out his professional qualifications and experience. The statement of experience should not be merely a string of generalities, but should emphasise experience in relevant and comparable fields. It is important to maintain a balance between undue modesty and overstatement. One occasionally hears statements of qualification and experience which are so overblown as to cause the tribunal to wonder why the witness is not the head of a leading world power or at least a famous international industrialist, rather than a

professional man giving evidence on a matter of no general importance. On the other hand false modesty is equally a temptation to be
avoided.

The form and matter of the proof from that point on will vary widely
according to the nature of the dispute and to the instructions given to
the witness, that is to say the matters on which he is required to give
evidence. There is however a general pattern which should be followed, namely that of stating the facts first and then giving the conclusions drawn from the facts and the reasons for arriving at those
conclusions.

In a typical case arising out of a contract for the construction of a
building, the facts would cover such matters as:

1. Details of the contract e.g.:
    (a) Date of its formation
    (b) Name of parties to the contract
    (c) Subject matter of the contract
    (d) Names of the professional advisers
    (e) Leading relevant particulars, such as the dates for possession
         of the site and for practical completion of the works
    (f) The contract conditions, referring to one of the various
         standard forms if applicable and the date of the edition
         concerned
    (g) The other contract documents, such as drawings, specifica-
         tion, bills of quantities
2. Brief history of the witness's instructions
3. Evidence of site inspections made setting out the matters referred
    to previously in Chapter 5
4. Detailed evidence of such matters as the state of completion of the
    building at the date of inspection, of measurements taken, and of
    other relevant matters such as particulars of materials on site
5. Evidence of work alleged to be defective

From there the proof would go on to deal with the method of valuation
of the work, stating the bases applied both as to measurement and as to
pricing, with reasons. If the valuation document takes the form of a
priced bill of quantities or some other such detailed document, this
would preferably be a separate document attached to the proof.

Reference should be made to the Scott Schedule if one has been
prepared, so that the witness can be taken through it item by item; this

may well involve giving detailed analyses of the valuation of some hundreds of items.

Next, the proof would set out the conclusions drawn from all that has gone before insofar as they are relevant to the matters in issue, again with the supporting reasons. If references to standard works are considered necessary, they should be given at the appropriate places in the proof.

The proof should then deal with the evidence of the opposing expert, as far as it can be deduced from the pleadings or has been examined in an exchange of reports, giving the reasons why the witness disagrees with it.

THE DRAFTING OF A PROOF OF EVIDENCE

What has been said previously in Chapter 5 should be re-emphasised in the drafting of a proof of evidence. As far as possible use short words and short sentences. Avoid technical language as far as possible, particularly when evidence will be given before a lay tribunal; a greater degree of technicality is permissible when the tribunal is known to possess technical expertise, such as an arbitrator appointed for that reason.

Above all, avoid generalities that cannot be maintained under cross-examination e.g. 'It is well known that . . .'; 'it is generally recognised that . . .'. A witness once stated in his proof 'It is well recorded that . . .' and went on to make statements that he was quite unable to sustain in cross-examination, with the result that the whole of his evidence was suspect, if not valueless.

The proof should be typed in double-spacing and must have wide margins for counsel's notes. Normally this is done on brief paper (or on the international size equivalent to brief known as A3) but foolscap (international equivalent A4) is also used. Paragraphs should be numbered and main and sub-headings given; pages must be numbered, and it is useful to give a reference in the top right-hand corner of each page. If the proof is of sufficient length to warrant it, a contents page may be given at the front, setting out the main and the sub-headings and the paragraph numbers to which these relate.

When a proof has been read and considered by the advocate it is likely that the witness will be called to a conference, when the proof will be gone through in detail. This can result in revisions to the proof, which may necessitate retyping the whole or parts of it.

EXAMPLES

The following are examples respectively of:

1. a report in a shipping case.
2. a proof of evidence in a construction case.
3. a proof of evidence in an insurance case.

They are practical examples based upon actual cases with certain details changed or omitted to avoid embarrassment. They do not necessarily conform in all respects with what has been said in this chapter. The examples are therefore not reproduced as models but rather to encourage the reader to analyse them for their good points and their shortcomings. Brief comments have been inserted at the end of each example as a guide.

EXAMPLE 1

Report on a shipping matter prepared for instructing solicitors by a consulting analytical chemist and biochemist.

Report on alleged damage to grapeseed extraction pellets carried in (name of ship), prepared by M.W. Drymouth BSc, PhD, FRIC, FBiol.

1. I have examined the various documents which you forwarded to me with your letter of 28 September 1979.

2. In order to put comments which I shall be making subsequently into context, I summarise briefly below the main items of information in the documents which I consider to be of relevance.

3. The vessel loaded 800 tonnes of grapeseed extraction pellets in bulk at Anzio between 22 and 24 September 1975.

4. Weather conditions at the time were hot and dry.

5. The cargo was delivered to the vessel in road trucks and was in apparent good order and condition at the time of loading.

6. Average samples were taken by cargo superintendents by mixing samples taken from each road truck.

7. They report that temperatures were checked during loading and were normal, but there is no information on the actual temperatures found. There is also no information on the precise ambient temperature at the time of loading, but presumably at maximum this would have been in the region of $25-30^{\circ}$C and it seems likely that the temperature of the cargo would have been similar to the average prevailing ambient temperature.

8. One of the five average loading samples was analysed by Messrs Jaca and Sangreso, who report moisture and oil contents of 12.1 per cent and 1.9 per cent respectively.

9. The vessel proceeded to Liverpool, where she arrived on 4 October; the cargo was discharged on 6 and 7 October.

10. I note from your letter that the vessel's single hold is fitted with four ventilators extreme forward and aft, the latter two having electric fans, and that the cargo was ventilated at all times during the voyage except between 30 September and 4 October. In the latter period heavy weather was encountered as confirmed by the Deck Log entries, and you state in your letter that the ventilators were closed off during this period to prevent ingress of water.

11. The reports of two local surveyors pertaining to discharge at Liverpool indicate that the surveyors concerned boarded the vessel on 7 October, the second day of discharge, when it appears that there were about 250 tonnes of cargo remaining on board.

12. Both survey reports confirm that:
    (a) There was no evidence of ingress of water into the hold.
    (b) At the time of the survey there were two areas of the stow located towards the after end of each of the two hatchways, where the cargo remaining on board was noted to be heating and affected by mould growth.

33

13. It appears that the cargo thus affected was not confined to the surface in the areas concerned but that heating, caking to some extent and microbiological growth was observed deeper within the stow. It is reported that about 249 tonnes were finally discharged from the vessel in a heated condition.

14. Regular inspections of the affected cargo were apparently carried out in the transit shed and the surveyors confirm that despite the fact that cargo was spread over a wide area of the shed floor and was turned over regularly, the pellets continued to exhibit self-heating.

15. A sample of sound and two samples of affected cargo taken from the discharged cargo were submitted for analysis and were found to have moisture contents of 12.74 per cent and 13.46/14.09 per cent respectively.

16. The underwriter's surveyor is of the opinion - and it is alleged in the Statement of Claim - that the damage was caused by inade-quate and/or improper ventilation. It is implied that the cargo should have been ventilated during the early part of the voyage when fair weather was encountered by raising the hatch boards.

17. On the other hand, the other local surveyor is of the opinion that the heating and resultant damage were directly associated with the inherent vice of the commodity.

    COMMENTS

18. On the question of ventilation it appears that the cargo was venti-lated at all times during the voyage when weather conditions were appropriate. As regards the inference that the cargo should have been ventilated during the early part of the voyage by raising the hatch boards, I would comment that in my experience this is entirely contrary to normal nautical and commercial practice and the only exception to this rule might be if the vessel had been specifically instructed to adopt such a practice when possible during the sea voyage.

19. From the description of the vessel's ventilating system given in your letter and the fact that the cargo was in bulk it is clear that ventilating air, when applied, would have passed over the

34

surface of rather than through the cargo. In my opinion, such
ventilation would have affected only the top layer of the bulk
stow to a depth of about 2-3 feet and would have had no significant
influence on the temperature or moisture content of cargo deeper
within the stow. Furthermore, if the hatch boards had been opened
during the early part of the voyage and, assuming the fans in the
aft ventilators had been on suction, the same total volume of air
would have been extracted, some being drawn through the forward
ventilator and some through the hatch covers. If the fans had been
blowing air into the holds, again the same total volume of air
would have been introduced into the cargo space, some leaving via
the hatchboards and some via the opposing natural ventilators. Thus
the net effect of opening the hatch covers would have been neglig-
ible provided the cargo was not stowed up into the coaming and,
even had this been the case, opening the corner hatch boards would
still only have had an effect on the top 2-3 feet of cargo.

20. From the data which is available it appears that at the time of
    discharge areas of heating cargo were found at considerable depths
    within the stow.

21. I propose to discuss the likely cause of the heating later, but
    in the light of my general knowledge and experience of bulk cargoes
    of the type in question, I am firmly of the opinion that the sur-
    face ventilation which was applied would not, and could not, have
    had any controlling influence on the heating within the stow; even
    if surface ventilation had been possible throughout the voyage,
    this situation would not have been altered.

22. In this respect it has to be borne in mind that a cargo of this
    type possesses relatively good insulating properties. Below a
    fairly thin outer layer and in those areas within the stow where
    no heating was occurring, the cargo at the time of discharge would
    have been essentially at the same temperature as at the time of
    loading. In the other areas where conditions were obviously favour-
    able for microbiological activity and associated self-heating to
    develop, there would have been no effective means for the heat
    produced to have been dissipated, thus leading to a gradual rise in
    temperature.

23. In view of the heating which developed within the stow, the surface ventilation which was applied may to some extent have helped to minimise ship's sweat formation. In any event, however, it would appear that ship's sweat formation could not have been a significant contributory factor to the damage which occurred.

24. One of the surveyors at Liverpool comments on condensation having been observed on 7 October on the vessel's steelwork but the other surveyor's remarks indicate that he observed no evidence of any significant sweat damage.

25. Since these surveyors were apparently not called to attend on board at the outset of discharge and were in attendance only after a considerable quantity of cargo had been discharged, it is to be presumed that there was no significant surface damage apparent when the hatches were first opened.

26. Quite clearly any damage due to ship's sweat would have been expected to have been distributed over the surface of the cargo and perhaps to a somewhat greater extent in the areas of the sides of the coamings. Any ship's sweat falling back onto the cargo would, furthermore, have been absorbed by the surface layer and in my view would not have penetrated the cargo to a depth greater than about 2 feet. Certainly, in my opinion, the phenomenon of sweat formation cannot explain the self-heating which was found at considerable depths within the stow.

27. There are two principal mechanisms via which self-heating can develop in cargoes of processed oil seed products:
    (a) Chemical oxidation of the residual oil in the cargo. The reactions involved here are exothermic, that is they are accompanied by the production of heat. Once such reactions start to occur within a stow the rate of increase in temperature is usually fairly rapid.
    (b) Microbiological activity. The observations of visible mould growth in parts of the cargo at the time of discharge and the fact that the degree of self-heating at the time of discharge was not excessive strongly suggest that the self-heating was probably entirely due to microbiological activity. Increases in temperature due to such microbiological activity can

initiate chemical oxidation reactions, but again in view of
the fact that heating was not excessive and also that the oil
content of this cargo was comparatively low, it seems unlikely
that oil oxidation played any significant role in the development of heating.

28. For microbiological growth to occur in a cargo of this type it is
generally considered that the moisture content and temperature of
the cargo must be such as to lead to an equilibrium relative
humidity of the atmosphere around the pellets of about 70 per cent
or above.

29. Based on my experience of cargoes of this general type I consider
that at normal temperatures of about 20°C, the critical moisture
content of the cargo above which microbiological activity and associated heating could develop would be about 13 per cent. At the
same temperature but with increasing moisture content above this
level, the risk and degree of microbiological heating would be
proportionately increased, since with increasing relative humidity
of the surrounding atmosphere the range and rate of proliferation
of indigenous micro-organisms which become capable of growth also
increases progressively.

30. I would also mention that since equilibrium relative humidity is
dependent on both moisture content and temperature, the critical
maximum moisture content of about 13 per cent as mentioned above
would increase with decreasing temperature of the cargo and would
decrease with increasing temperature of the cargo.

31. In the case of this particular cargo, it is evident from analysis
of the loading sample that the average moisture content of the
consignment was 12.1 per cent. However, there can be little doubt ✻
that the moisture content of individual truck-loads would have
varied quite considerably, perhaps by 2 per cent or more, about
this figure.

32. Pelletisation usually involves compression, and the use of live
steam followed by cooling of the resultant pellets and process
control is often such that final moisture contents cannot be pre-
cisely controlled and may vary by a few per cent.

The Expert Witness

33. In this case, on the basis of the data available it can be concluded that the moisture content of certain truck-loads which
were loaded on the vessel must have been sufficiently in excess
of the average figure determined by analysis for the observed
microbiological activity and associated heating to have developed
in transit, given the likely temperatures prevailing in the cargo
at the time of loading.

34. It will be noted from my previous comments that if, as assumed, the
temperature of the cargo at the time of loading was about 25-30°C,
and portions of the cargo as loaded had in fact moisture contents
of about 13 per cent or above, microbiological activity and heating would be expected. In this respect the moisture contents of
13.46/14.09 per cent found in samples of the damaged cargo discharged are entirely consistent with the heating observed.

35. Quite clearly unless the heating cargo which was deposited in the
transit shed was turned at frequent enough intervals so that the
heat produced within the pile could be dissipated at a faster rate
than it was evolved, the temperature in the pile would continue to
increase, or at least would not diminish.

36. I would comment finally on analytical data pertaining to various
other shipments of the same type of cargo which were included with
the documents supplied and which were attached to a letter dated
9 December 1976 from the cargo owners' solicitors. The date indi-
cates average moisture contents ranging from 11.0-15.77 per cent
for these various shipments and in the letter it is stated that
in none of these cases was the cargo in any way defective.

37. It will be evident from my previous comments that at least for
those shipments which apparently had average moisture contents of
14.4-15.77 per cent, I am rather surprised that no heating damage
developed during transit. However, I would reiterate that the
development of microbiological heating is dependent not only on
moisture content but also on temperature. Furthermore, given suitable conditions of moisture content and temperature for microbiological activity to occur, associated increases in temperature will
be progressive with time.

38

38. For the other shipments referred to above there is no information on temperatures of the cargo at loading or the length of the voyages between loading and discharge. I note, however, that most of these shipments were of Spanish origin.

39. It is of course possible that in certain cases the moisture content/temperature of pockets of these shipments may have been at or above the critical level for microbiological growth to have occurred. However, if the moisture content/temperature had been at or very near to the critical level, microbiological activity and associated heating would have been relatively slow and depending on the lengths of the voyages in question, it is possible that associated damage may not have progressed either to a noticeable extent or to a level at which receivers of the cargo considered any damage to be significant.

Signed .... M. W. Drymouth

Date .... 23 November 1979

Comment

Does the reader consider that certain phrases e.g. 'there can be little doubt' (par. 31) and 'may vary' (par. 32) are justified in the light of the remainder of the report?

EXAMPLE 2

Proof of evidence of a consulting engineer in a construction case. This concerned an underground boiler house which was a cause of dispute. The case, heard by an arbitrator, was in a sense one of 'Hamlet without the prince'. The contractor was claiming the balance of money alleged to be due for work done and the employer's defence alleged defective work, the cost of remedying which would exceed the contractor's claim. The contractor said that any defects arose from defective design by the architect engaged by the employer and not from defective workmanship or materials. The architect declined to be joined in the proceedings. Mr. Harlington was commissioned by the employer to report on certain aspects of the case.

The Expert Witness

Mr. D.K. Harlington will say:

1. I am a chartered engineer, a member of the Institution of Civil Engineers and a member of the Institute of Water Engineers. I have had thirty years' experience in civil and structural engineering, on the contracting side and latterly in practice as a consulting engineer. I have had extensive experience of reinforced concrete structures, particularly those that have to withstand water pressure.

2. In accordance with instructions given me by Messrs. Hardy and Freeman, Solicitors for the Respondents, I visited the Respondents' factory on 7 October 1969 and examined the basement boiler house and storage tank chambers.

3. My first reaction was one of surprise that such an installation could have reached almost completion without serious thought being given to the necessity of amending the original design, which, apparently, has been followed in spite of the difficulties experienced in carrying out the work.

4. It would appear to me that:
   (a) right from the start no consideration was given to the question of fire precautions.
   (b) no steps were taken prior to the start of the work to ascertain the exact dimensions of the plant to be installed.
   (c) no proper calculations were made when designing the chambers in respect of the strength of the walls and of the correct materials to be used for them.

5. Regarding the first point, the installation as designed allowed for the storage tank and boiler to be in the same compartment, the dimensions of this chamber being such that very little room could be allowed between the two units. The only access to the chamber allowed was by means of the manhole situated inside the building above. The objections of the Fire Authorities to the proposed layout made it necessary to construct a wall between the storage tank and boiler, and to form an outside manhole with cat-ladder for access to the boiler room.

40

6. The first essential of any installation involving boilers is the provision of clear and adequate means of quick exit. Almost as important is the protection of fuel storage against the risk of fire. Neither of these points, apparently, were given any consideration at any stage of the design.

7. With the amendments insisted upon by the Fire Authorities, the installation could hardly be more inconvenient. Access to the now totally enclosed storage tank is virtually impossible, and even if a man were prepared to take the risk and succeeded in gaining access through the manhole opening, the very confined space would prevent him from doing anything useful in the chamber. Should the tank rust or spring a leak, I cannot imagine how maintenance or remedial work would be carried out upon it.

8. With regard to the boiler, this is also in a very confined space which will make proper maintenance on it extremely difficult.

9. Turning to the second point, my previous remarks regarding the serious shortage of working space around the plant shows that, in plan, the original design could not have been based upon any accurate dimensions of the units. Equally serious, from a convenience point of view, is the fact that the depth of the chamber below ground level was about two feet less than it should be. It was the intention to have the top of the roof slab over the chamber at the same level as the floor of the building above it. When the tank and boiler were placed in position, it was discovered that the chamber was too shallow and consequently the roof over them had to be raised nearly two feet above the floor of the superstructure. The access steps to this higher level have defeated the whole object of having a completely level floor.

10. The last point may be considered the most important of the three, as the whole safety of the installation depends upon the proper design of the underground chamber. The floor of this chamber is about 8 feet below ground level; the walls of it are built in common bricks $13\frac{1}{2}$ inches thick and jointed in cement mortar.

11. From the time the excavation for the chamber was carried out, trouble has been experienced continually from the subsoil water.

41

The presence of this ground water should have immediately indicated to those responsible that a change in the design of the floor and walls of the chamber was vitally necessary to ensure a sound and watertight job.

12. Even without the pressure of ground water, the 13½ inch thick brick walls can readily be shown theoretically to be of insufficient thickness to withstand earth pressure at 3 feet depth. Under an external pressure of 8 feet of water the conditions are even worse.

13. Regarding the materials used in the walls, it is my opinion that common bricks should never have been used. If brickwork were insisted upon, first quality engineering bricks should have been specified. However, owing to the serious ground water conditions, the walls should have been re-designed in waterproof concrete, and should have been in mass concrete of sufficient thickness or, preferably, in reinforced concrete. The floor, which also has to withstand the maximum upward water pressure, should have been suitably reinforced.

14. Ample evidence that the walls are unable to retain the external water has been given on a number of occasions. In an attempt to make the walls watertight, Sealocrete rendering has been applied to the walls internally. This has proved to be of little use, as the rendering has been forced away from the wall face by the water pressure. It need hardly be said that the continual seepage of water through the walls must have the effect of weakening them as, being in brickwork, they cannot have the same resistance as a monolithic concrete wall would have.

15. I have been informed that a drain has been proposed to relieve the ground water pressure around the chamber. Levels will permit this to drain the water away to within about 2 feet 6 inches above the chamber floor. This certainly would reduce the water pressure considerably. The thickening of the walls of the boiler house, at their base, may help to withstand the substantially reduced water pressure when the drain is in, but it is my opinion that it is of little use under present conditions.

16. Bearing in mind all the causes of concern when considering the
     general aspect of the matter, if a completely satisfactory instal-
     lation is to be insisted upon, I can see no method of attaining
     this, other than by scrapping the underground chambers entirely and
     replacing them with a properly designed building on the surface. If
     it is decided that this should be avoided if possible, I would
     suggest that:

     (a) The boiler should be removed from its present position.

     (b) The division wall between boiler and tank should be removed.

     (c) The larger chamber thus formed should house the storage tank
          only, placing it so that there is adequate room around it.

     (d) A new underground chamber be constructed outside the end of
          the building above, to house the boiler, this chamber to be
          sited so as to allow a convenient flue connection between
          boiler and chimney stack. The chamber to be properly designed
          and constructed to withstand external pressures, from what-
          ever cause, and to be completely watertight. Access to this
          chamber to be made by a flight of steps, suitably protected
          against the weather.

     (e) The access manhole to the storage tank compartment also to be
          protected from the weather. A cantilever roof from the wall
          of the building above could also be arranged so as to protect
          both the manhole and steps.

     (f) If proved to be necessary, the walls of the storage tank
          chamber could be strengthened internally. The extra room in
          the bigger chamber should allow this to be done.

17. In making the above suggestions it has been assumed that the drain
     will be laid to relieve most of the water pressure. When this is
     done, the tank chamber could be rendered in Sealocrete around all
     the walls.

Comment:

1. Paras. 2 and 3.
    How did the witness know all this from the visit alone?
    Should he not enlarge on how he reached this conclusion?

2. Para. 5.
   'Proposed layout.' What layout was this, when prepared and by whom?
3. Para. 9 (a).
   'Original design.' No reference is made to drawings examined.
   (b). 'the roof . . . had to be raised.' How does the witness know this?
4. Para 11
   'trouble has been experienced.' How does the witness know this?

EXAMPLE 3

Proof of evidence of an insurance consultant. The case consists of a claim under an interruption insurance policy, the dispute being over the trend of the business during the indemnity period.

Mr. T.C. Diggory will say:

1. I am a fellow of the Chartered Insurance Institute, a member of the education and training committee of that Institute, and a Vice-President of the London Insurance Institute. I am the author of the standard textbook 'Principles and Practice of Interruption Insurance' and of several treatises and articles to the technical press on this subject. I am now an Independent Consultant on Insurance with particular reference to Interruption Insurance matters. I was, until becoming a consultant some seven years ago, an underwriter in this field of insurance being Consequential Loss Manager for the Resistant Assurance Co Ltd for a number of years.

2. I have considered Exhibit A which comprises a standard United Kingdom Consequential Loss or Interruption insurance policy made out in the name of the Plaintiff as insured and the Defendants as insurers. The term Interruption has replaced that of Consequential Loss in the last few years and the recognition of this is shown by the corresponding change of syllabus title in the Chartered Insurance Institute Examinations. It reduces misunderstandings still further from the older generic references to this class of business as Profits Insurance, Loss of Profits Insurance, Consequential Loss and sometimes Pecuniary Loss insurance.

3. Loss of gross profit is the main item of cover under the Interruption policy. The basis of the quantum of the cover given by the gross profit item of the policy is one stated as being 'as indemnity'.

4. The insurance contract is really in two parts.

5. The preamble or opening page of the document, apart from dealing with preliminary matters and the payment of premium, requires the happening of an insured contingency at the stated premises and for the trading of the business to be interrupted thereby. This can be regarded as 'triggering' the policy into operations. The preamble also subsequently stipulates that the damage must have arisen from a contingency for which there was insurance in respect of material damage and that payment has been made or agreed will be made thereunder. This is called the 'material damage warranty'. Subject to these requirements being met i.e., an insured peril and admission of such claim by material damage insurers, the quantum of the insurance protection is set out in the Specification to the policy.

7. The Insured in this case at the time of the loss had cover in force under a single gross profit item defined as including the total Payroll for the sum of £5 million, with an eighteen months' maximum Indemnity period and relating to his business as a Nut and Bolt manufacturer carried on at his two factories and other premises in the United Kingdom, all as stated in the policy.

8. The Specification sets out a number of definitions which allow for the main statement of the method of calculating the loss to be uncluttered with such matter. It will be seen that three of the definitions are subject to what is often called the 'bracketed provisions' - merely indicative of the typing or layout - more correctly called 'the special provisions' providing for the adjustment of the particular terms, if necessary, to give a more correct assessment of the loss. The key to it is in the last phrase 'so that the figures thus adjusted shall represent as nearly as may be reasonably practical the results which but for the damage would have obtained during the relative period after the damage'.

9. While not specifically provided, it is the usual practice to determine the quantum loss without such adjustments. Thus the history

45

of trading for the corresponding period of the year in which interference to the business has taken place will be matters of fact in the business records of the Insured and the actual trading done will also be recorded for the period affected by the damage together with a record of the increased costs of working expended. So, if no adjustment arose, the calculation could be made from factual information and if this is done, then it is easier from such a factual base to discuss the various factors which may involve adjustments to be made to reach 'the would-have-been position'.

10. I think it is important to stress this procedure as it also determines the onus of proof and the extent to which this has to be established on the parties. It also clearly establishes that the quantum assessment can be varied, in fact should be varied, to give the 'would-have-been result'. From the evidence that has been agreed and certified as correct, the position would be as set out in Exhibit 41 if no adjustment arose to the claim from the basis of historic figures.

11. The Specification wording then deals with savings in insured standing charges, increased costs of working and any adjustment necessary if there has been underinsurance. Thus is established the initial loss amount arising but we need then to consider what variation factors arise ie the provision of the 'other circumstances' clause.

12. I should mention that in the older wording of this clause the word 'special' appeared but as this seemed to overstress the meaning it is replaced as you will see in line 5 with the word 'other'. The adjustment is needed to deal with all the factors that have changed if the comparison with the previous financial trading position is to produce a proper indemnity. I have taken the figures as provided by Mr. Abacus the Accountant and the adjustments submitted by Mr. Midas the Financial Director and Exhibit 41 sets out the quantum calculation arising in accordance with the policy terms.

13. The first item restricts the quantum to that arising in consequence of 'reduction in turnover' of the business. This can be in the form of the financial amount arising from such reduction or

what might be termed 'salvage costs' which have avoided such loss, called increased costs of working.

14. The operation of the calculation of the quantum is specifically set down in the Specification and it is important to proceed in that form. The basis is to compare the trading within the actual indemnity period (which must not exceed the maximum insured) with the corresponding period in the twelve months of the last financial year. Thus is established the initial shortfall in turnover. To this is applied the Rate of Gross Profit as determined from the last financial year's accounts and this establishes the initial Gross Profit loss.

15. The Policy wording provisions - calculation of quantum of loss - are Item 1 The rate of gross profit applied to the fall in turnover for the indemnity period together with the increased costs of working to minimise a greater loss (these latter figures have been agreed).
   In figures this is 40 per cent of £200 000 shortfall in the six months out of the twenty-four months indemnity period of cover that was affected by the fire damage, ie arithmetically £80 000.

16. I deduce however from the evidence of Mr. Abacus that from his investigations of the operation of the business both before, during and after the affected indemnity period, the business was expanding at about 15 per cent per annum and that in consequence the shortfall in turnover should be assessed at £280 000. Further as this extra trading has been possible without proportional increase in employees the rate of gross profit that would have been earned has to be dealt with as 45 per cent. Thus the arithmetical calculation of the loss now becomes 45 per cent of £280 000 ie £126 000.

17. There are further adjustments to be made relative to:
   (a)   savings in standing charges   £500
         and
   (b)   increased costs of workings £12 500
   but these have been agreed and are not at issue. They are shown in Exhibit 41 accordingly making the actual calculation at this stage £126 000 less £500 plus £12 500 ie £138 000.

47

18. I would however accept that following such adjustments it is neces-
     sary to reconsider the adequacy of the existing sum insured of
     £2 000 000.

19. On the basis of the rate of gross profit of 45 per cent and adopt-
     ing the 15 per cent trend for the twelve months from the date of
     the fire to give the 'would-have-been' level of trading turnover
     of £2 300 000 the sum insured required for full cover is 45 per
     cent x £2 300 000 times two as the indemnity period is two years
     ie £2 070 000. Thus while without the adjustment as stated, the
     sum insured was adequate, it is now slightly below what is neces-
     sary and the amount payable of £138 000 is reduced by the ratio
     2 000/2 070 = £133 333.33.

20. The defendants have claimed that the adjustment should be carried
     forward over the whole maximum insured indemnity period of twenty
     four months and not on the position of growth limited at twelve
     months from the date of the fire.

21. I would draw attention to the Definitions in the Specification to the
     policy. These relate to the historic figures i.e. those of the last
     financial year and which have been agreed and are therefore not in
     issue. The key definition is Annual Gross Profit and on the first
     page of the Specification, against item 1 at the end of the wording,
     there are the provisions for underinsurance or, as it is referred to,
     proportional reduction. The precise wording is: "provided that if the
     sum insured by this item be less than the sum insured produced by
     applying the Rate of Gross Profit to twice the Annual Turnover, the
     amount payable under this item shall be proportionately reduced".

22. I submit that my calculation is on this basis and it is not correct
     to bring in any further adjustment.

Comment:

1. Paras. 7, 14 and 15.
    Does the witness make the question of the indemnity period clear,
    in view of the varying periods mentioned?
2. Paras. 15 and 16
    Is the relation between the two rates of gross profit sufficiently
    explained, and is it clear how the figure of £280,00 is arrived at?

Chapter 7 Preparation of the Case: Documentation

In many technical cases, except perhaps those involving medical evidence or evidence on commodities ('looksniff' cases as Lord Justice Donaldson once succinctly described the latter) there is a mass of documents of all kinds to be examined, considered and taken into account by the expert witness. It is imperative that he should make himself thoroughly familiar with all the documents that bear on his aspect of the case at the earliest possible moment. Failure to do so may at a later stage reveal fatal flaws in his evidence.

Documents provided by instructing solicitors often arrive as mere unsorted bundles. They should if necessary be sorted into categories, e.g. correspondence, invoices, test records and so on so that the important points of the case can be more easily assimilated. If there is a large mass of correspondence it may be worthwhile to prepare an index under various subject headings: this has been found invaluable in complicated cases, particularly where the correspondence has stretched over a period of years.

If a case concerns a contract issued on a printed standard form, the expert must always ask to see the actual contract deed, and never use a blank copy of the standard form. Instructions may be gloriously vague as to the contract deed, and may in construction cases merely use a phrase such as 'the 1963 JCT Form', without specifying which of those forms is exactly the one referred to, quite apart from the question of the numerous amendments which the form has undergone since 1963 and the fact that the printed form may have been amended by agreement between the parties. It is therefore essential to see the actual document signed by the parties with the contract conditions attached.

Typical examples of documents that may need examination in construction cases are as follows:

1. Contract deed and conditions
2. Specification
3. Bills of quantities
4. Contract drawings
5. Other drawings issued during the course of the works
6. Instructions issued by the architect or engineer
7. Sub-contractors' and suppliers' estimates and accounts
8. Invoices
9. Daywork sheets
10. Clerks of works' and foreman's diaries
11. Records of hidden work
12. Correspondence
13. The final account

It can be a daunting task to be faced with a great mass of documents and to have to absorb them in what often seems to be a totally inadequate space of time but that is the lot of the expert and it is a vitally important part of his duty.

THE PREPARATION OF DOCUMENTS FOR THE HEARING

It is of great assistance to a tribunal for an agreed bundle, or agreed bundles, of documents to be prepared before the hearing. Such a bundle would be fastened together in the top left-hand corner and the pages numbered consecutively. In this way reference can be made quickly and with certainty by counsel saying e.g., 'I turn now to letter No. 86 in the bundle'. If, as often happens, there is a great mass of correspondence extending over a period of years to be considered it can be of assistance to have a separate bundle enclosed in covers of a distinctive colour for each year's correspondence. The use of ring binders for fastening the bundles can be a considerable convenience. Sometimes the bundles are certified as having been agreed by the parties to be put in evidence. The numbering should be done by a numbering machine for the sake of clarity; hastily scrawled numbers can be a great source of frustration.

If there is a large number of documents to be put in it is useful to split them up into categories, e.g. correspondence, contract documents, drawings, invoices, daywork sheets and so on. In such a case each bundle would bear a distinctive letter as well as having the contents numbered, so that for example a drawing could bear the reference H3, it being the third item in bundle H.

Four sets of documents are normally required – one for the tribunal, one for witnesses and one for each party. The preparation of the agreed bundles is normally a matter for the solicitors on both sides, but experts may be asked to advise on this aspect of a case.

Maps and plans should be folded and not rolled. It does not assist the smooth conduct of proceedings for a tribunal to be constantly wrestling with drawings which roll themselves up the moment they are released. They should be folded, bearing the identifying reference both on the face of the document when opened out and on the outside when folded. All maps and plans generally should have a north point marked on.

If photographs are produced they should bear a label on the face giving a brief description of what is seen and the date that it was taken. Again it does not help the tribunal to have to keep turning a photograph over in order to read on the back what it is all about. What is worse is to have produced a set of photographs each bearing only a number. Either the tribunal has laboriously to write on the description; to adjourn the proceedings while this is being done, or to interrupt counsel continually in order to be reminded of the missing description.

A better method is to have the photographs (if there is any number of them) bound in book form with a fold-out index attached to the back for easy reference. In addition a site plan should be prepared indicating the point at which each photograph was taken and the direction in which the camera was pointing. Each point on the plan should then be marked with the reference number of the relevant photograph.

An expert will often find it of great assistance to take photographs on his original site inspections but it may well be that at a later stage he will need instructions from the solicitors in order to employ a professional photographer if photographs are to be put in evidence.

Old documents may be of considerable value in a case, such as drawings deposited with a local authority for planning or bye-law approval. These may still be obtainable, although the reorganisation

51

of local government appears to have played havoc with records in certain cases.

If an expert is to produce documents or other exhibits himself he should mark each one with a prefix and a number. The prefix (which could be in the form of his initials) will identify the document as being one which he has himself produced, and which he may be called upon to prove at the hearing. What has been said above about documents generally applies equally to documents produced by a witness.

Chapter 8   The Scott Schedule

The Scott or Official Referee's schedule is a document used in proceedings such as construction disputes in which there are many detailed items in issue. It sets out briefly in tabular form the contentions of the parties in regard to each of the items in dispute and it offers a convenient method of dealing with the items without having to refer to several separate documents. If properly prepared and used it can save much time, trouble (and occasionally temper) at a hearing. The schedule may also be valuable in reducing the scope of the dispute as the parties may agree over a large number of small items when seeing them set out in this form, as opposed to their being buried away in a mass of documents. The costs of an action can form such a formidable factor in the ultimate result that any legitimate procedure or device such as the Scott schedule should be employed wherever appropriate in order to clarify matters for the tribunal and thus to reduce costs.

The Scott schedule may be required arising from an order of the court or of an arbitrator made at a preliminary meeting. The form of the schedule may be varied to suit the particular requirements for a case; in those proceedings where there is a counterclaim, there may be two schedules, one dealing with the items in the claim and the other dealing with the counterclaim. The actual form of the schedule may be agreed between the parties, or may be specified by the official referee, or by an arbitrator in arbitration proceedings.

Typical examples of the layout of a Scott schedule are given below, prepared for use in a hearing before an arbitrator. In a case heard before an Official Referee, the terms plaintiff, defendant and Official Referee would be substituted for claimant, respondent and arbitrator respectively.

EXAMPLE 1. CLAIM BY CONTRACTOR FOR EXTRAS

This format is suitable for those cases in which the contractor is claiming for extra works or extra items of cost which are disputed by the employer. The contractor as claimant will complete columns 1–5 and the employer as respondent will complete columns 6 and 7. Columns 8 and 9 are left for the arbitrator to complete either at the hearing or during the drafting of his award, as may be appropriate. Adequate space should be given to the matter to be included in the various columns: Nothing is worse than an ill-presented schedule that cannot be clearly and instantly read and understood. Instead of assisting the tribunal it may have the very reverse effect.

Column 1 gives the serial number for reference purposes.

In Column 2 are given references to relevant documents, such as bills of quantities or specifications. In appropriate cases reference might be made by number to a drawing, to a clause in the contract conditions, to an architect's or engineer's instruction or to other relevant document.

In Column 3 is set out a brief description of the extra works or extra items of costs claimed.

In Column 4 the claimant will give comments in support of his claim for the item and in Column 5 the price he is claiming. The latter may be shown merely as a lump sum or may be shown in the form of a calculation, e.g. 5 weeks at £100.00 per week = £500.00.

In Column 6 the respondent will set out his comments as to why the item should not be allowed, and Column 7 would then be completed by the word 'Nil'.

Alternatively, the item may be accepted in principle but contested as to price. In this case some such wording as 'Agreed subject to price' would appear in Column 6, and the respondent's offer would be given in Column 7.

It is a convenience for the price columns to be cast through to the end of the schedule, coming to totals agreeing with the figures given in the pleadings.

If the respondent has a counterclaim arising, for example, from a dispute over the determination of the employment of a contractor, then he should prepare a separate schedule headed 'respondent's counterclaim'. The column headings would follow those given in Example 1 with 'respondent' substituted for 'claimant' and vice versa. The respondent would complete Colums 1 to 5 and the claimant Colums 6 and 7.

EXAMPLE 1. CLAIM BY CONTRACTOR FOR EXTRAS

1	2	3	4	5	6	7	8	9
Item No.	Reference	Description	Claimant's Comments	Claimant's Price	Respondent's Comments	Respondent's Price	Arbitrator's Comments	Arbitrator's Sum awarded
15	Architect's instruction No. 4 (ii)	Extra scaffolding for raising height of boundary wall	The Scaffolding had to be re-erected because A. I. No. 4 (ii) was not issued until after the original scaffolding had been struck	£500.00	Claimant comments denied. See Clerk of Work's report No 10.	NIL		

EXAMPLE 2. ITEMS DISPUTED ON A REMEASUREMENT CONTRACT

This format is suitable for dealing with disputes arising on a type of contract which provides for the whole of the work to be remeasured on completion and valued at rates set out in a schedule of rates. Columns 1 to 7 would be completed by the claimant and Columns 8 to 11 by the respondent. Columns 12 and 13 are left for the arbitrator. In Column 9 the quantity claimed is shown as agreed 'as figures', that is to say, without admission of liability. This narrows the field of dispute within this particular item, as previously explained.

EXAMPLE 3. DEFECTS ALLEGED BY EMPLOYER

This format can be used in those cases where the employer counter-claims against the contract sum for defects of materials and/or workmanship and for work not carried out.

Columns 1 to 5 would be completed by the respondent, Columns 6 and 7 by the claimant and Columns 8 and 9 by the arbitrator. The comments under the heading of Example 1 can be repeated here for Columns 1, 2 and 3. In Column 4 the respondent states the basis of his counterclaim and in Column 5 the cost of remedying the defective work. In those cases where it is not appropriate physically to renew the defective work in all the circumstances involved, a respondent may accept the work as it stands with the proviso that he counterclaims for the diminution in value of the work as a whole.

In Column 6 the claimant says why he disputes the item. Column 7 may be completed as shown or a sum may be inserted 'subject to liability'.

Scott v Avery Clause

A Scott Schedule is not to be confused with a Scott v Avery clause, i.e. a provision in an arbitration agreement making the arbitrator's award a condition precedent to the commencement of an action in the courts. The two things are totally distinct and unrelated.

EXAMPLE 2. ITEMS DISPUTED ON A REMEASUREMENT CONTRACT

1	2	3	Claimant's				Respondent's				Arbitrator's	
			4	5	6	7	8	9	10	11	12	13
Item No.	Reference in Schedule of Rates	Description	Comments	Quantity	Unit Rate	Sum claimed	Comments	Quantity	Unit Rate	Sum offered	Comments	Sum awarded
9	Item 7/C	Extra for excavation in rock to basement	This required com-pressed air plant	435 m³	£10.00	£4350.00	This was not rock within the contract definition	435m³ 'agreed as figures'	NIL	NIL		

EXAMPLE 3. DEFECTS ALLEGED BY EMPLOYER

1	2	3	4	5	6	7	8	9
			Respondent's		Claimant's		Arbitrator's	
Item No.	Reference	Description	Comments	Cost of remedial work	Comments	Sum offered	Comments	Sum awarded
6	Specification P. 17	Granolithic paving	The paving dusted badly and is unacceptable	£246.00	The paving was executed strictly in accordance with Specification	NIL		

Chapter 9　The Hearing: General Procedure

Procedure at the hearing varies according to the type of tribunal before whom the matter is heard. Civil cases in Court follow more or less a set pattern and those heard by arbitrators are usually on the same lines, except that a considerable degree of flexibility of procedure may be employed according to the circumstances of the case. These may vary from the 'looksniff' type of case in which the arbitrator relies solely on his own knowledge and experience to the full-dress case involving counsel, solicitors and witnesses, including experts. In this and the succeeding chapter procedure in the latter type of case is described.

Counsel for the plaintiff (or the claimant, in arbitration proceedings) makes his opening address by reading the pleadings and giving a general picture of the matters in issue and setting out in clear terms what his client seeks by way of remedy for the wrongs he considers he has suffered at the hands of the defendant (or the respondent, in arbitration proceedings). He then calls his first witness and takes him through his proof of evidence in question and answer form. This is known as examination-in-chief. When this is concluded counsel for the defendant cross-examines the witness. Again, when this is over, counsel for the plaintiff may ask further questions, and this procedure is known as re-examination. There are marked differences between these three forms of examination and each will be dealt with separately at a later stage.

The witnesses for the plaintiff are all dealt with in this manner and when the last witness has been dealt with counsel will indicate to the tribunal that he has concluded his case by some such phrase as 'That is the case for the plaintiff'.

The order in which witnesses are called is entirely a matter for counsel. He may start with lay witnesses, followed by expert witnesses who have been pre-involved in the case, and then call 'independent' expert witnesses. There may be occasions when witnesses are, with the agreement of the tribunal, taken out of order, that is to say, an expert for the defendant on a particular part of the case may immediately follow the plaintiff's expert on that same matter. This again is a matter for counsel, but with the consent of the tribunal.

It is then the turn of the defendant. His counsel may make an opening address or he may decide to proceed straightaway to the examination of his witnesses. These are dealt with in turn in exactly the same manner as those of the plaintiff, namely examination-in-chief, cross-examination and re-examination. When they have all been dealt with counsel will indicate that his case is completed.

The order of things is then reversed, counsel for the defendant making his closing address first, followed by the closing address for the plaintiff.

The judge (in a non-jury case) will then either give his judgment immediately or he will reserve it and deliver it on a later named day. In the case of arbitration it is usual for the arbitrator to reserve his judgment, which is in the form of a written document known as the award.

A typical form of procedure has been outlined, but it must be appreciated that an expert witness may only be present for a part of the time i.e. to give his own evidence and to hear that of the expert or experts for the other side. The latter is done so that he can advise counsel through the instructing solicitor on points that arise during the examination of the opposing witnesses. The other reason for this sporadic attendance is of course the question of costs. Experts are expensive and their time should not be avoidably wasted.

Counsel appearing as advocate has been used in the foregoing example, but this is by no means invariable. The courts have rules as to rights of audience, that is to say, who may represent the parties. For instance solicitors have a right of audience in certain courts, while in others only counsel may appear. There is however no restriction on audience before an arbitrator: a party may be represented by counsel, by a solicitor, in person or by another lay person.

Appearance as a witness in court can be something of an ordeal, at any rate until a witness is experienced. The bullying of witnesses is now largely a thing of the past, but nevertheless witnesses can be roughly treated at the hands of a severe advocate. It is a useful thing for a witness who knows that he is to be called to give evidence to attend a court hearing beforehand so as to get accustomed to the surroundings, the general atmosphere and the procedure. Even the robes of judge and advocates can appear strange and vaguely disturbing to the un-accustomed witness. Lord Justice Donaldson has said, 'The plain fact is that people tend to be frightened of courts and judges. There are interesting arguments for and against the retention of our traditional judicial dress, but no one has ever suggested that robes and a wig make a wearer look particularly human or understanding'.*

Procedure in front of tribunals other than the courts may be less formal. It is not customary in arbitration proceedings, for example, for the advocates to appear robed.

Hearings usually start at about 10.30 am and finish at about 4.30 pm, with an adjournment of about an hour for lunch. This may seem a short working day but five hours in the witness box can be just as tiring for the witness as for counsel and, moreover, for a judge or an arbi-trator who has to concentrate on every word and make notes. Lord Roskill has said, 'Do remember the wisdom of the judicial five-hour day. Exhaustion can all too easily lead to error by advocates, arbi-trators and judges alike'.† This applies equally to witnesses.

HINTS FOR THE EXPERT WITNESS

Some general hints for the witness may not be out of place. These may appear trivial, but experience has taught that, when taken and acted upon, they will materially assist in giving evidence to the best effect.

Personal appearance. A neat appearance will give a good impres-sion; an unkempt, untidy appearance will not only give the opposite impression but may be regarded as showing a lack of respect for the tribunal. Remember Polonius's advice to Laertes, 'For the apparel oft proclaims the man'.

Be relaxed. If you are required to stand to give evidence, stand with feet apart, with weight evenly balanced. Do not fidget from one leg to another. If the examination is prolonged, ask if you may sit. If per-mission is given, do not loll in the chair. This gives a bad impression

---

* In a paper to the annual conference of the Chartered Institute of Arbitrators, 1978.
† In the Alexander lecture to the Chartered Institute of Arbitrators, 1977.

and may be regarded as disrespectful to the tribunal. Relaxation will assist concentration, and this is essential all the time a witness is giving evidence. Concentration may flag in the course of a long cross-examination, and relaxation will help to combat this.

Speak clearly and at a reasonable speed. No-one upsets a judge and counsel more rapidly than a mumbling witness who has to be continually reminded to speak up. Again, this shows a lack of courtesy and respect to the tribunal.

Speak both to the tribunal and to counsel questioning you. Courts are arranged so that this can be done without difficulty, but it is not always so in less formal proceedings.

Watch the pen of the judge or whoever is conducting the proceedings and adjust the pace of your answer to his note-taking. Witnesses who insist on speaking both at length and at great speed may well find that the tribunal has abandoned note-taking out of desperation and exhaustion and the benefit of their rhetoric is lost. A provincial counsel (we will call him Jones) earned the soubriquet of 'Pause-there-a-moment-Jones' because all the time the witness was answering his questions he had one eye on the judge's pen and he regulated the speed of the witness's answer to the note-taking of the judge by the cautionary remark that earned him his nickname. It may have been overdone, but if so it was a good fault.

Answer questions clearly and briefly, provided that the substance of the question is covered. Never be afraid to answer 'Yes' or 'No' if that is all that is required by the question. Avoid verbosity and repetition. A regrettable tendency that appears to be growing rapidly is for witnesses to give answers of totally unnecessary length, much of which is irrelevant or merely repetitious. As an example, a witness was once heard to reply to a question which clearly called for the one word 'Yes' in answer say instead, 'I go along with the philosophy of those sentiments'. An even worse example was:- 'On a full consideration of the matter in issue I have reached the final conclusion that the answer should on balance be in the affirmative'. Whatever the cause, such verbosity is to be deplored. Apart from the debasement of language, it wastes the time of the tribunal and detracts from the value of the evidence being given.

Two experts were giving evidence on the same rather limited aspect of a case, and it had been agreed that they should be taken one after the other, that is to say, the second one (appearing for the defence) was taken during the presentation of the plaintiff's case. The reasons for this are not here relevant. The first witness was garrulous, and often irrelevant in his evidence, despite all attempts by his own counsel to bring him to heel. Examination-in-chief, cross-examination and re-examination took over an hour and a half. The second witness was clear, direct and very much to the point, and he was only twenty minutes in the witness box. Needless to say, his evidence made a very much greater impact on the tribunal than that of his long-winded, meandering opponent.

Use clear terms, preferably in language understood by the layman, even when before a technical tribunal such as an arbitrator chosen for his professional expertise and experience. The use of unnecessary jargon is not only merely annoying, it may even serve to confuse the tribunal. Thus, a heating engineer giving evidence as to what would happen when certain adjustments were made to a domestic heating installation said, 'The temperature of the room would become severely depressed'. What he meant was, 'The room would become much colder'. So why not say so? Again, this same witness spoke of 'a marked decay in temperature'. Decay, in the sense of decomposition, is often accompanied by the generation of heat, and further questions had to be asked to make it clear that the witness meant a fall in temperature when he used the term 'decay'. His original reply was ambiguous, whereas the use of plain, clear English would have made his meaning immediately clear and beyond doubt.

An example of the mistake of saying more than one need in answering is provided by the case of the woman being cross-examined in a divorce case. This occurred in the days when adultery needed to be proved in such cases. She was asked if she had ever committed adultery on the back seat of a certain make of car. She replied quickly and firmly 'No'. There was a very slight pause and then, without any prompting, she added, 'You can't anyway. It's too small'. This led on to prolonged further questioning which did much to destroy her earlier evidence.

There may be occasions when a witness is pressed by counsel merely to answer 'Yes' or 'No'. If, however, the witness considers that a point is being dealt with inadequately, or even misleadingly, by such an answer, he should follow his terse monosyllable by a request to the tribunal, 'May I enlarge on this point?' Permission being given, he can then expound his view as he considers fit.

Avoid the pert answer, the attempt to repartee, when being cross-examined. The expert is (or should be) master of his own expertise, but counsel is (or should be) master too of his own expertise, one very important part of which is the art of examination. An expert who does try to score off counsel will in all probability come to regret it later on when counsel, by his expertise in examination, has floored him. The point made by the witness in a firm yet courteous manner will always get home. Counsel will tacitly acknowledge the position by making a non-committal remark such as 'very good' (when he really means the opposite) and moving on to the next point of attack.

Avoid mannerisms. One can fall into mannerisms quite unknowingly during a lengthy period of examination. They should be avoided, because they can become a source of irritation to the tribunal.

An expert witness – a quantity surveyor – in a construction case in the High Court once succumbed to this temptation in the course of a lengthy time in the witness box. He developed early on two mannerisms. One was to take an interminable time to answer the most simple question, and the other was constantly to repeat the phrase 'And that was another example of how I bent over backwards to be fair to the contractor'. These mannerisms caused increasing irritation to the judge, a fact of which the witness appeared blissfully unaware. When immediately before the luncheon adjournment one day he paused for what seemed an eternity while searching for an answer to a perfectly strightforward question, the judge's patience finally gave out. Without waiting for the witness to speak he said with icy calm, 'I imagine that in this instance you not only bent over backwards to be fair to the contractor but ended up flat on your face as well. The court will adjourn till 2.15 pm.'

A further mannerism to be avoided is that of repeating at length each question as put, before answering it. This kind of thing is all too common:

Q   Did you visit the site on October 15th?
A   Did I visit the site on October 15th? Yes I did.
Q   When you visited the site on October 15th did you meet Mr. Jones, the contractor's surveyor, by appointment?
A   When I visited the site on October 15th did I meet Mr. Jones, the Contractor's surveyor, by appointment? Yes, I did. We had a standing arrangement.
Q   When you were at the site that day did you prepare a valuation of the work executed and the materials on site?
A   When I was at the site that day did I prepare a valuation of the work executed and the materials on site? (Pause) Yes, I did.

Q   Did you agree that valuation there and then with Mr. Jones?
A   Did I agree that valuation there and then with Mr. Jones? Yes, I
    did.
Q   Is Document No 321 in the bundle a copy of the valuation?
A   Is Document No 321 in the bundle a copy of that valuation?
    (Pause while the witness thumbs through the bundle). Yes, it is.

And so on and on and on, hour after gruelling hour. Apart from the
totally unnecessary waste of time (and consequent cost) it can be
infuriating to all concerned, counsel and tribunal alike.

The necessity for concentration has been referred to and this is
particularly important when, during a long cross-examination,
counsel may try to trap a witness into an admission that may weaken,
or even destroy, his evidence. An example of loss of concentration and
the disastrous effect it has on an expert's testimony occurred in the
County Court some years ago, in a case about alterations to a farm-
house.

The builder was suing for the balance of his account; the defendant's
case was that the builder's charges were unreasonably high.

The builder's expert, a quantity surveyor, had given his opinion very
firmly that no-one who had not seen the premises before the work was
carried out as well as after it had been could possibly assess the value of
the work. He was strongly pressed on this in cross-examination,
counsel's line of attack being that an experienced quantity surveyor
such as the witness could surely measure and value building work of
any type. The witness stuck staunchly to his opinion that this
particular work could not be valued, and counsel could not budge him.

Then counsel proceeded to question the witness on the details of the
builder's account.

This set out the hours worked, and the materials and plant used –
the normal type of daywork account. When cross-examined on this,
the witness followed the line of his original contention in that he said
that he could not vouch for the number of hours worked, the quantities of the various materials used, or the hours charged for the different
items of plant. What he did say was that the unit rates charged for
labour, materials and plant were all reasonable. Thus his evidence,
though limited, was perfectly consistent and counsel had not been able
to fault him.

The second part of the cross-examination had been taken at a
leisurely pace very different from that of the brisk opening encounter

and counsel expressed his appreciation of the helpful way in which the witness had given his evidence.

Then the trap was set. Counsel, in a disarming way, said, 'Well, Mr. Brown you have studied this matter most thoroughly in all its aspects and I am sure you must have formed some conclusion about it. How much do you think this work is really worth?' and the witness said 'I think it was worth x thousand pounds'. The trap had been sprung and the witness, out of his own mouth, had virtually destroyed the whole of his evidence. A few sharp closing questions for counsel did the rest.

A witness should always keep calm even if he considers that opposing counsel is being unfair or even provocative in the questions he is putting. If a witness fails to do so he may well give answers that he would not give in calmer moments. Thus the value of his evidence will be called in question and he may lose the respect of the tribunal. A witness who loses that respect can do great harm to his client's case.

If a witness cannot answer a question he should say so. He can always ask for time to consider the matter. If one the other hand he hazards a guess and is proved wrong it may cast doubt on the rest of his testimony. Guesswork is not in the province of the expert witness. Similarly if he has made a mistake in his evidence (and in long, complicated technical matters a mistake can slip through despite the greatest care being taken) he should admit it without hesitation. There may be a reasonable explanation of how the mistake came to be made or it may on the face of it not be capable of explanation. Whichever it is, the witness must own to it straightaway. The tribunal is likely to be impressed by the honesty of a witness who is prepared to admit an error. The remainder of his evidence may well carry greater conviction as a result.

Chapter 10   The Hearing: Detailed Procedure

The procedure generally followed before the Courts and in certain types of arbitration proceedings has been given in outline in the preceding chapter and it will now be examined in more detail.

OATH-TAKING

A witness giving evidence in the courts (the High Court, Crown Courts, County Courts, and Magistrates' Courts) must do so on oath or affirmation. By Sub-section 3 of Section 12 of the Arbitration Act 1950 'An arbitrator or umpire shall, unless a contrary intention is expressed in the arbitration agreement, have power to administer oaths to, or take the affirmations of, the parties to and witnesses on a reference under the agreement'. Evidence before the Lands Tribunal must be given on oath or affirmation. In quasi-judicial proceedings and at administrative inquiries it is not usual for witnesses to be sworn, though the power exists in certain cases.

The manner of taking the oath normally used in the courts is as follows. The witness takes the New Testament or, in the case of a Jew the Old Testament, in his uplifted hand and says or repeats after the officer administering the oath the words 'I swear by Almighty God that the evidence I shall give shall be the truth, the whole truth and nothing but the truth'. Persons of other religious faiths are sworn in a manner binding on their conscience.

If a person has no religious belief, or if his religious belief precludes him from swearing an oath he may be allowed to affirm. The prescribed form of affirmation is:

'I, A. B., do solemnly, sincerely and truly declare and affirm that the evidence I shall give shall be the truth, the whole truth and nothing but the truth'.

EXAMINATION-IN-CHIEF

The witness is taken through his examination-in-chief by the advocate who has called him. This examination, in question and answer form, is normally based upon the witness's proof of evidence and the witness therefore knows the lines that the questioning will take. With certain exceptions, leading questions are not permitted in examination-in-chief. Leading questions are those that anticipate the witness's reply and may be regarded as putting words into his mouth. For example, a question, 'The roof was leaking, wasn't it, when you inspected the property?' may not be put in examination-in-chief. A suitable form would be 'What was the state of the roof when you inspected the property?'

The exceptions to the rule about leading questions are that they may be permitted to identify the witness and give his qualifications and experience. For example, counsel may start the examination-in-chief by saying to the witness: 'You are John Brown, of 6 The Ridings, Watchford, Essex, a Fellow of the Chartered Insurance Institute. You have practised for some twenty years on your own account mainly in London and the Home Counties as a fire loss assessor on claims dealing with domestic, commercial and industrial buildings'. Leading questions may be permitted in civil cases in respect of agreed and uncontroversial material, such as the identification of documents. This saves the time of the tribunal. In addition the parties in civil proceedings can agree to a witness being 'led'.

Practice varies as to the way in which a proof of evidence is dealt with at the hearing. In the superior courts and before certain tribunals an expert witness is not allowed to read from his proof or to take it into the witness box. In less formal proceedings, such as an arbitration hearing, this may be allowed if the other party agrees; such agreement may be conditional upon the opposing party being provided with a copy of the proof. At planning enquiries it is common practice for an expert to be allowed to read his proof to the tribunal as his examination-in-chief, copies having been furnished to the tribunal and to the opposing side.

The advantages arising from the use of a proof of evidence in examination-in-chief are that the witness does not have to rely on his memory in regard to matters that took place some time before; his evidence on facts and figures similarly does not become an exercise in memory-searching and is therefore more reliable. Also it can materially reduce the time taken by the examination-in-chief of the witness. The variation of practice by different tribunals makes it important for the witness to ascertain beforehand whether it is proposed that his proof is to be handed in or not, because this may well affect the way in which the proof is drafted. The refusal of certain tribunals to allow a proof of evidence to be taken into the witness box does not however preclude reference by the witness to notes and to copies of documents relevant to the matters in issue. It is however advisable always to seek the tribunal's permission to do so before referring to any documents.

An expert may refer to standard works and recognised authorities to confirm his opinion. He may also refresh his memory by notes he made at the time of the events on which he is giving evidence; for example, he may refer to his own diary.

At the close of the examination-in-chief the advocate who called him will use a phrase such as, 'Please wait there, Mr Brown' indicating that he has completed his examination of the witness, and opposing counsel will then cross-examine.

CROSS-EXAMINATION

Cross-examination is an important part of proceedings conducted in the legal system derived from English common law, known as the adversarial system. Its purpose is to test the truth of a witness and the accuracy and completeness of his evidence, and in doing so to weaken or destroy the opposing case and thus to establish the case of the party for whom it is conducted.

Counsel is not required to cross-examine and if the evidence-in-chief is not disputed there is no point in doing so. Evidence given by an expert is likely to be controversial and failure by counsel to cross-examine would be taken as an admission of the points made by the expert in his examination-in-chief. Leading questions are permitted in cross-examination, but counsel may not impugn the character of an expert witness. Subject to that the witness's credibility may be attacked e.g. his knowledge of the facts, his impartiality, his truthfulness, the basis on which he founded his conclusions.

A searching cross-examination can be a severe test of an expert's own knowledge and experience and he must be prepared for this. He must also be ready to answer questions which though perhaps not apparently directly relevant to the matters in issue may be admitted by the tribunal. Thus in a famous murder trial many years ago an expert, a metallurgist, was called by the defence to give evidence as to the cause of destruction by fire of a motor-car. His evidence contradicted the case being presented by the prosecution. The opening question put to him in cross-examination was, 'What is the coefficient of expansion of brass?' The witness replied, 'I do not know'. The question was put in identical form twice more, and on each occasion produced the same answer. Thus at the very outset the credibility of the witness was severely attacked for lack of knowledge.

An expert undergoing cross-examination should not yield to the temptation put to him by counsel to make a mental calculation. However capable a man may be, to produce an accurate answer while the whole Court watches him in silence as he cudgels his brains may prove too much of a test and a wrong answer given under these circumstances may tend to vitiate otherwise unimpeachable evidence. The witness should instead ask leave of the tribunal to do what is required of him at the next adjournment. An expert in a building dispute had quoted to him prices for some half-dozen or so items of work and was asked to comment on them. The judge interposed by remarking that the witness could not be expected to answer such a question. Quite undeterred counsel then asked, 'Presumably you could go into the matter at the luncheon adjournment'. The witness replied, 'It would take some hours of detailed work' and counsel did not pursue the point.

A witness under cross-examination must remain incommunicado, that is to say he must not discuss the case during an adjournment with counsel, solicitors, professional colleagues or anyone at all. This may give rise to difficulties, particularly during a prolonged cross-examination, if points arise on which discussion would be helpful, but the rule admits of no avoidance.

Cross-examination may appear to be, and may in certain cases actually become, an ordeal, particularly to a person inexperienced in giving evidence. However, if an expert has prepared his case thoroughly and if he sticks at all times to the truth as he sees it, cross-examination should hold no fears for him. Counsel is trained and experienced in questioning, but the expert has the advantage that the battle, if it be regarded as such, is conducted in the realm of his own knowledge and experience.

RE-EXAMINATION

At the close of cross-examination, the witness may be re-examined by counsel who conducted his examination-in-chief. The purpose, and the limit, of re-examination, is the elucidation of points raised in cross-examination. No new matters may be introduced, and if this is done the opposing party will be given an opportunity to cross-examine on those matters. As in examination-in-chief, leading questions may not be put to a witness. If the evidence of the expert has not been upset to any extent by cross-examination, counsel may decide not to re-examine.

RECALL OF WITNESSES

A judge may recall a witness either at his own instance or that of a party for further examination or cross-examination and similar powers are exercised by other tribunals. If a witness is recalled by a judge he may be cross-examined only by leave of the judge.

EXAMINATION BY TRIBUNAL

The expert must be prepared to answer questions raised by a judge, an arbitrator or other person conducting the proceedings or, in certain circumstances, a jury. If such questions are interposed during counsel's examination of a witness, at whatever stage of his evidence, they can be a source of difficulty to counsel, disturbing his line of questioning. The Rt. Hon. Lord Denning, Master of the Rolls has said 'The judge's part . . ., is to hearken to the evidence, only himself asking questions of witnesses when it is necessary to clear up any point that has been overlooked or left obscure; to see that the advocates behave themselves seemly and keep to the rules laid down by law; to exclude irrelevancies and discourage repetition; to make sure by wise intervention that he follows the points that the advocates are making and can assess their worth; and at the end to make up his mind where the truth lies. If he goes beyond this, he drops the mantle of a judge and assumes the robe of an advocate; and the change does not become him well'.*

An example of judicial intervention breaking the thread of an advocate's questioning occurred in a case arising out of a building contract. The case was a fairly long one, with experts on both sides. The judge appeared to take every opportunity to interrupt counsel in order to put questions on his own line of thought, often at considerable length. This happened to counsel on both sides of the case to their increasing frustration. One particular morning an expert was subjected to such questioning lasting half an hour or so in the middle of his examination-in-chief. Eventually counsel was allowed to resume and the examination-in-chief was still in progress at the luncheon adjournment. On the witness asking whether he could eat with others involved in the case or whether he should eat alone, junior counsel turned to his leader and said, 'He can eat with us, can't he. He's not being cross-examined'. At this the leader, remembering the exasperation caused by the judge's intervention, snarled at his junior, 'And what do you think has been going on all this morning'

OTHER DUTIES AT THE HEARING

Experts are allowed to be present throughout the hearing in civil cases and an expert may therefore be required to attend during the examination of the other party's expert witness in the same area. This entails closely following the evidence and making notes of any points that may assist either in the cross-examination of the opposing expert or in his own examination-in-chief. These should be kept for conferences during adjournments. However, if points arise which in his opinion need dealing with there and then he should pass notes to the instructing solicitor who will then decide whether or not to interrupt counsel. In proceedings less formal than those of the Courts, counsel sometimes find themselves bombarded with notes from solicitors and experts. This practice interrupts the thread of counsel's examination which in turn tends to break the concentration of the witness, and it should therefore be avoided or kept to a minimum.

If daily transcripts of the proceedings are made available to the parties within a comparatively short time of the tribunal rising, the

---

* *Jones v National Coal Board* [1957] 2QB55.

expert must be available to examine the opposing expert's evidence in detail and bring to the attention of his instructing solicitor points which he considers should be pursued.

Other duties of a more onerous nature may fall to the expert during a hearing.

Judges, inspectors, and those generally who conduct proceedings have a habit of issuing commands at inconvenient times. While these are normally couched in delicate terms such as, for example, 'No doubt these figures can be prepared during the luncheon adjournment' or 'it will be a convenience to have these particulars ready for the resumption first thing tomorrow morning' they are nevertheless instructions that have to be obeyed. This can involve the expert in working at high pressure without any notice and often at considerable personal inconvenience. He may be required to produce new details, either on his own or in collaboration with the opposing expert according to the circumstances of the case, with the attendant risk of error which may lead to difficulties, particularly if he is cross-examined on these new items. Nevertheless, this is a hazard that has to be faced.

Another and even greater difficulty can arise from the production by the other side of documentary evidence in the shape, for example, of detailed drawings. These will need to be studied, assessed and criticised by the expert and this in all probability will involve his working long and late on them. This in turn may necessitate his making amendments to his proof of evidence, having the proof or parts of it retyped, and conferring with counsel on the alterations. The benefit lies in counsel's ability to deal with these new points in examination-in-chief and thus possibly taking the sting out of cross-examination. The dangers, however, are all too evident; owing to the pressure under which this work is done, errors may appear on the face of the proof, and the balance of a well thought-out proof may be upset by undue emphasis on these last-minute matters. Despite the pressure of time the greatest care should be taken over any such last-minute alterations.

THE TRIBUNAL'S VIEW OF THE EXPERT

Apart from dealing with the technical aspects of an expert's evidence, the tribunal in its judgment may comment on the impression created by the expert when giving evidence. Such comments may be favourable or critical, on occasion highly so. The criteria applied by the tribunal are those of impartiality and helpfulness. If an expert is palpably unable to draw a fair conclusion or if his evidence is given in such a way that it does not assist the tribunal to come to a fair decision then he is merely wasting the time of everyone concerned.

Chapter 11   Summing-up

An expert witness is likely to hear only a part of a case in which he is instructed. Experts are expensive people and attendance at a trial or hearing tends to be kept to a minimum in terms of time if only for that reason. Apart from giving his own evidence, an expert's attendance may be limited to hearing the evidence of the opposing expert and advising on how points made in the course of that evidence can best be dealt with.

As a result the expert may fail to get a balanced picture of the case as a whole. For this reason, it is helpful to obtain a transcript of the judgment, or a copy of the award in arbitration proceedings. (Since the passing of the Arbitration Act 1979, reasoned awards are likely to become the rule rather than the exception that they have been in certain types of case so far). A study of the judgment or award can be a valuable guide for the future, as with hindsight (once defined as the most exact science known to man) the expert can ponder on how he played his part. Happy is the man who can say with complete conviction that he would not have altered any of his evidence; the expert witness of normal fallibility – and blessed with a measure of humility – may well feel that there were parts of his evidence that could with advantage have been given differently.

It is always pleasant to be on the winning side but the important thing is to be satisfied that one has acted honestly and fairly. It is not unknown for a witness who has created a good impression (whatever the result of the case) to be instructed later on by the party against whom he originally appeared.

The settlement of disputes by an independent tribunal – whatever form that tribunal may take – is one of the marks of a civilised society.

Lord Roskill has said, 'So long as human nature is what it is there will always be disputes. And those disputes, whatever their character, must be resolved, if society is to exist in a civilised way, as quickly, as cheaply, and as satisfactorily as possible'.* The expert witness who, by proper use of his knowledge and experience, assists in that process, is playing an important role in the maintenance of that free and civilised society.

To sum up, therefore, the duties of the expert witness are as follows. First, to assist the tribunal to the best of his ability by giving his evidence truthfully and fairly while at the same time doing his duty to his client. Second, to fulfil the duties which he owes both to himself, that is to his own conscience and to the maintenance of his own credibility, and also to his chosen profession or calling in maintaining its standards.

* In the Alexander lecture to the Chartered Institute of Arbitrators, 1977.

Appendix A
Glossary of Legal Terms
(Adapted from Osborn's Concise Law Dictionary)

Action A proceeding commenced by writ or in such other manner as may be prescribed by rules of court, to enforce a civil right.

Admissions Statements, oral, written, or inferred from conduct, made in evidence by or on behalf of a party to a suit, and bearing to the truth of a fact against himself.

Affidavit A written statement in the name of a person, called the deponent, by whom it is voluntarily signed and sworn to or affirmed.

Attested copy A copy of a document which is certified correct by a person who has examined it.

Certiorari An order commanding an inferior court of record to remove proceedings into a superior court for judicial review.

Common law That part of the law of England formulated, developed and administered by the old common law courts, based originally on the unwritten common customs of the country.

Construction The process of ascertaining the meaning of a written document. The judicial interpretation of statutes.

Contra proferentem The doctrine that the construction least favourable to the person putting forward an instrument should be adopted against him.

Counterclaim   A counterclaim may be made by a defendant who alleges that he has any claim, or is entitled to any relief or remedy against a plaintiff, instead of bringing a separate action.

Defence   A pleading served in any action in reply to the statement of claim.

Defendant   A person against whom an action, complaint or other civil proceeding (other than a petition) is brought, it may also be a person charged with an offence. In arbitration proceedings the person against whom the action is brought is known as the respondent.

Deposition   A statement on oath of a witness in a judicial proceeding; the evidence of witnesses before a magistrate or justices taken down in writing. It may be signed both by the witness and at least one of the committing magistrates.

Directions, summons for.   The purpose of this summons is to obtain directions for the discovery and inspection of documents, the mode and place of the trial etc.

Discovery of documents   In actions begun by writ, lists of documents relating to the action which are or have been in each party's possession must be served by each party after close of pleadings, and any party entitled to have discovery may serve a notice requiring an affidavit verifying the list of documents. Also, in any action, however begun, the court may order any party to make and serve a list of documents, and may order him to make a verifying affidavit.

Document   See Sec. 10(1) of the Civil Evidence Act 1968 (See Appendix C).

Equity   Equity is the body of rules formulated and administered by the Court of Chancery to supplement the rules and procedure of the common law. The rules of equity are administered in all divisions of the Supreme Court and where there is any conflict between the rules of law and of equity, equity is to prevail.

Exparte   An application in a judicial proceeding made: (1) on behalf of an interested person who is not a party to the action; (2) by one party in the absence of the other.

Hostile witness   A witness whose mind discloses a bias adverse to the party examining him and who may, with leave of the court, be cross-examined by the counsel calling him.

Interlocutory proceeding   One which is ancillary to the main action. Thus, interlocutory applications in an action are only intermediate steps and do not finally decide the action.

Judicial notice   The courts take cognisance or notice of matters which are so notorious or clearly established that formal evidence of their existence is unnecessary: ie matters of common knowledge and every-day life.

Particulars   The details of the claim or the defence in an action which are necessary in order to enable the other side to know what case they have to meet. 'Further and better particulars' may be ordered at the discretion of the court.

Per curiam   By the court.

Per incuriam   A decision of the court which is mistaken. 'What is meant by giving a decision per incuriam is giving a decision when a case or statute has not been brought to the attention of the court and they have given the decision in ignorance or forgetfulness of the existence of that case or that statute'. *Huddersfield Police Authority* v *Watson* [1947] 2 All ER 193, per Lord Goddard CJ at p. 196.

Plaint   The written statement of an action brought in the county court.

Plaintiff   One who brings an action at law. In arbitration proceedings the one who brings an action is known as the claimant.

Privilege   In the law of evidence, the following matters are protected from disclosure on the grounds of privilege: (1) professional confidences; (2) matrimonial communications; (3) criminating questions.

Puisne   A puisne judge means a judge of the High Court of Justice other than the Lord Chancellor, the Lord Chief Justice of England, and the President of the Family Division. The puisne judges are styled 'Justices of the High Court'.

Recitals   Statements introduced to explain or lead up to the operative part of an instrument. They are generally divided into narrative recitals, which set forth the facts on which the instrument is based; and introductory recitals, which explain the motive for the operative part. A recital normally commences with 'Whereas'.

Referee   A person to whom a question is referred for his decision or opinion; an arbitrator. Official referees were appointed under the Administration of Justice Act 1956, but the office was abolished by the Courts Act 1971, s.25 and the functions of official referees are discharged by circuit judges.

Service of process   A writ of summons and all other originating processes must be served effectively, i.e., personally, or by post or by acceptance of service by the defendant's solicitor.

Submission   A submission to arbitration is an instrument by which a dispute or question is referred to arbitration pursuant to an agreement between the parties. For the Arbitration Acts to apply it must be in writing.

Subpoena   A writ issued in an action or suit requiring the person to whom it is directed to be present at a specified place and time, and for a specified purpose, under a penalty (*subpoena*). The varieties in use are: (1) the *subpoena ad testificandum*, used for the purpose of compelling a witness to attend and give evidence; (2) the *subpoena duces tecum*, used to compel a witness to attend in court or before an examiner or referee, to give evidence and also bring with him certain documents in his possession specified in the *subpoena*.

Tort   A civil wrong for which the remedy is a common law action for damages, and which is not exclusively the breach of a contract, or the breach of a trust or other merely equitable obligation.

Appendix B
Types of Tribunal

(Taken from 'General Principles of English Law'
by Redmond.)

THE JUDICIAL SYSTEM

The judicial system is organised into a hierarchy of courts as follows:

1.   The European Court of Justice

The passing of the European Communities Act 1972 involved that 'all
rights, powers, liabilities, obligations and restrictions. . . . under the
Treaties, and all remedies and procedures under the Treaties. . . . are to
be given legal effect in the United Kingdom.'
   By virtue of this statute:

   (a)   Certain provisions become part of, and even prevail over,
         English Law.
   (b)   Matters relating to the meaning or effect of the Treaties or of
         any other community instrument must be referred to the
         European Court, or, if not, decided in accordance with the
         principles laid down in that Court.

The Court has nine judges and four Advocates-General.

2.   The House of Lords

When sitting as a court only the Law Lords – the Lords of Appeal in
Ordinary – are allowed to take part; together with the Lord
Chancellor, and any peer who holds or has held high judicial office,
e.g. a former Lord Chancellor.

Precedents of the House of Lords Appeals Committee are absolutely binding on all other courts in the United Kingdom (except the Judicial Committee of the Privy Council).

A precedent of the House of Lords can be overruled only by:

(a)   an Act of Parliament; or
(b)   a subsequent decision of the House of Lords itself.

3.   The Judicial Committee of the Privy Council

This consists of the Lord President of the Council (who rarely in fact participates), the Lord Chancellor, and a number of Privy Councillors. The Judicial Committee is the supreme court of appeal:

(a)   for Colonies and certain Commonwealth nations;
(b)   for the English ecclesiastical courts of the Church of England;
(c)   for appeals from medical tribunals; and
(d)   for appeals from the Admiralty Court of the Queen's Bench Division acting as a prize court.

A precedent of the Judicial Committee is binding on all courts in the territory from which the particular appeal was remitted.

Its precedents are not binding upon territories other than the one from which the appeal came; nor upon British courts.

4.   The Supreme Court

Consisting of the Court of Appeal and the High Court.

(a)   *The Court of Appeal*
This court ranks next below the House of Lords in the domestic structure.

It now has two divisions:

(i)   the Civil Division, which hears civil appeals from all divisions of the High Court, and the county courts;
(ii) the Criminal Division, which hears appeals from the Crown Court.

(i). The Civil Division
The Court is staffed by the Master of the Rolls and sixteen Lords Justices of Appeal. In addition the Lord Chancellor (and former Lord Chancellors), the Lord Chief Justice, the President of the Family Division and the law lords are ex officio members of the court, and the Lord Chancellor has power to co-opt High Court judges from time to time.

(ii) The Criminal Division
The Court is composed of the Lord Chief Justice and Lords Justices of Appeal, but the Lord Chief Justice (in consultation with the Master of the Rolls) may from time to time require judges of the Queen's Bench Division of the High Court to join the court.

(b) *The High Court.*
The High Court consists of three divisions: the Queen's Bench Division, the Chancery Division and the Family Division. All three divisions have an appellate function, and the more important appeals are heard by Divisional Courts of two or three judges sitting together.

(*i*) The Queen's Bench Division
This division consists of the Lord Chief Justice and puisne judges.
 As a Divisional Court, it hears certain appeals from the Crown Court and magistrates' court, and exercises supervisory jurisdiction generally by means of prerogative orders.
 The ordinary court deals with all classes of civil litigation not assigned expressly to other divisions e.g., actions in tort and contract.
 As the Admiralty court it deals with shipping matters such as salvage and exercises prize jurisdiction relating to seizure of vessels.
 As the Commercial Court it deals with certain specialised commercial disputes.
 The practice of the High Court in cases involving a large number of detailed items such as are common in disputes on building contracts is to refer such cases to judges who perform the function of 'Official Referees' for a report in accordance with Order 36 of the Rules of the Supreme Court (RSC). Under Order 36 (8) RSC matters may be referred with the consent of the parties to a Special Referee.

(*ii*) The Chancery Division
This division deals principally with the matters of Equity previously

dealt with by the old Court of Chancery, such as trusts. The division consists of the Vice Chancellor and puisne judges.

(*iii*) The Family Division

This court consists of a President and puisne judges whose jurisdiction covers non-contentious or formal probate matters; matrimonial causes; adoption, and guardianship of minors; and some inheritance claims.

5.   The Crown Court

The Courts Act 1971 abolished the old quarter sessional and assize courts, which formerly dealt with indictable offences, and transferred this jurisdiction to the new Crown Court. This consists of a jury and a judge appointed from among High Court judges, circuit judges and recorders (who are barristers or solicitors of at least ten years' standing, acting as part-time judges).

6.   The County Courts

County Courts deal with civil matters where the sum involved falls below a certain limit or where a statute confers jurisdiction (e.g., the Rent Acts). Normally appeal lies to the Court of Appeal, but bankruptcy appeals go to a Divisional Court of the Chancery Division. As a result of reorganisation effected by the Courts Act 1971, county court judges have been replaced by circuit judges, each of whom may serve several county courts and may (where necessary) move from one circuit to another. The County Courts have powers similar to those of the High Court to appoint Special Referees to hear matters. Much County Court work is involved with family matters.

7. Magistrates' Courts

Magistrates' Courts primarily deal with criminal offences. The Courts are presided over either by unpaid lay magistrates appointed by the Lord Chancellor and assisted by a legally qualified clerk of the court, or by a stipendiary magistrate appointed by the Lord Chancellor. Juvenile courts are presided over by specially qualified lay magistrates to deal with juvenile offenders and cases involving the care of children.

In addition magistrates' courts have a civil jurisdiction, mostly concerned with domestic proceedings.

8. Coroners' Courts

These are presided over by a specially qualified coroner (usually a doctor or a lawyer) assisted by a jury. The functions of the court are to inquire into the causes of any death where these were not immediately apparent, or where the death was violent or unnatural. The courts also hold inquests into the ownership of treasure trove.

STATUTORY TRIBUNALS

The function composition and procedure of statutory tribunals are governed by the relevant statutes and rules. Examples of statutory tribunals are as follows:

The Lands Tribunal
The Industrial Tribunals
Tribunals appointed to hear planning inquiries
Public Local Inquiries in Compulsory Purchase Orders
Rent Tribunals
Rating Tribunals
Tribunals appointed to deal with matters of taxation
National Insurance Tribunals
National Health Service Tribunals

PARLIAMENTARY INQUIRIES AND COMMISSIONS

These are set up ad hoc by Parliament, who lay down the terms of reference, the composition of the tribunal and its powers in relation to such matters as the calling of witnesses.

ARBITRATION

Arbitration may be defined as the process whereby two parties in dispute appoint a tribunal of their own choice (or accept a tribunal appointed under an agreed procedure) to settle the dispute. The majority of arbitrations are held in private on terms agreed by the parties, subject in England and Wales to the Arbitration Acts of 1950 and 1979. The enforcement of foreign awards is governed by the Arbitration Act of 1975.

Certain types of arbitration may take place by order of the High Court and others because they are ordained by statute.

Appendix C
(Legal Appendix)

CIVIL EVIDENCE ACT 1968

Part I

Hearsay evidence to be admissible only by virtue of this Act and other statutory provisions, or by agreement.

1. (1) In any civil proceedings a statement other than one made by a person while giving oral evidence in those proceedings shall be admissible as evidence of any fact stated therein to the extent that it is so admissible by virtue of any provision of this Part of this Act or by virtue of any other statutory provision or by agreement of the parties, but not otherwise.

    (2) In this section 'statutory provision' means any provision contained in, or in an instrument made under, this or any other Act, including any Act passed after this Act.

Admissibility of out-of-court statements as evidence of facts stated.

2. (1) In any civil proceedings a statement made, whether orally or in a document or otherwise, by any person, whether called as a witness in those proceedings or not, shall, subject to this section and to rules of court, be admissible as evidence of any fact stated therein of which direct oral evidence by him would be admissible.

    (2) Where in any civil proceedings a party desiring to give a statement in evidence by virtue of this section has called or

intends to call as a witness in the proceedings the person by whom the statement was made, the statement

(a) shall not be given in evidence by virtue of this section on behalf of that party without the leave of the court; and

(b) without prejudice to paragraph (a) above, shall not be given in evidence by virtue of this section on behalf of that party before the conclusion of the examination-in-chief of the person by whom it was made, except

   (*i*) where before that person is called the court allows evidence of the making of the statement to be given on behalf of that party by some other person; or

   (*ii*) in so far as the court allows the person by whom the statement was made to narrate it in the course of his examination-in-chief on the ground that to prevent him from doing so would adversely affect the intelligibility of his evidence.

(3) Where in any civil proceedings a statement which was made otherwise than in a document is admissible by virtue of this section, no evidence other than direct oral evidence by the person who made the statement or any person who heard or otherwise perceived it being made shall be admissible for the purpose of proving it:

   Provided that if the statement in question was made by a person while giving oral evidence in some other legal proceedings (whether civil or criminal), it may be proved in any manner authorised by the court.

Witness's previous statement, if proved, to be evidence of facts stated.
1865 c. 18.

3. (1) Where in any civil proceedings

(a) a previous inconsistent or contradictory statement made by a person called as a witness in those proceedings is proved by virtue of section 3, 4 or 5 of the Criminal. Procedure Act 1865; or

(b) a previous statement made by a person called as aforesaid is proved for the purpose of rebutting a suggestion that his evidence has been fabricated, that statement shall by virtue of this subsection be admissible as evidence of any fact stated therein of which direct oral evidence by him would be admissible.

(2) Nothing in this Act shall affect any of the rules of law relating to the circumstances in which, where a person called as a witness in any civil proceedings is cross-examined on a document used by him to refresh his memory, that document may be made evidence in those proceedings; and where a document or any part of a document is received in evidence in any such proceedings by virtue of any such rule of law, any statement made in that document or part by the person using the document to refresh his memory shall by virtue of this subsection be admissible as evidence of any fact stated therein of which direct oral evidence by him would be admissible.

Admissibility of certain records as evidence of facts stated.

4. (1) Without prejudice to section 5 of this Act, in any civil proceedings a statement contained in a document shall, subject to this section and to rules of court, be admissible as evidence of any fact stated therein of which direct oral evidence would be admissible, if the document is, or forms part of, a record compiled by a person acting under a duty from information which was supplied by a person (whether acting under a duty or not) who had, or may reasonably be supposed to have had, personal knowledge of the matters dealt with in that information and which, if not supplied by that person to the compiler of the record directly, was supplied by him to the compiler of the record indirectly through one or more intermediaries each acting under a duty.

(2) Where in any civil proceedings a party desiring to give a statement in evidence by virtue of this section has called or intends to call as a witness in the proceedings the person who originally supplied the information from which the record containing the statement was compiled, the statement

(a) shall not be given in evidence by virtue of this section on behalf of that party without the leave of the court; and

(b) without prejudice to paragraph (a) above, shall not without the leave of the court be given in evidence by virtue of this section on behalf of that party before the conclusion of the examination-in-chief of the person who originally supplied the said information.

(3) Any reference in this section to a person acting under a duty includes a reference to a person acting in the course of any trade, business, profession or other occupation in which he is engaged or employed or for the purposes of any paid or unpaid office held by him.

Admissibility of statements produced by computers.

5. (1) In any civil proceedings a statement contained in a document produced by a computer shall, subject to rules of court, be admissible as evidence of any fact stated therein of which direct oral evidence would be admissible, if it is shown that the conditions mentioned in subsection (2) below are satisfied in relation to the statement and computer in question.

(2) The said conditions are:

(a) that the document containing the statement was produced by the computer during a period over which the computer was used regularly to store or process information for the purposes of any activities regularly carried on over that period, whether for profit or not, by any body, whether corporate or not, or by any individual;

(b) that over that period there was regularly supplied to the computer in the ordinary course of those activities information of the kind contained in the statement or of the kind from which the information so contained is derived;

(c) that throughout the material part of that period the computer was operating properly or, if not, that any respect in which it was not operating properly or was out of operation during that part of that period was not such as to affect the production of the document or the accuracy of its contents; and

(d)   that the information contained in the statement reproduces or is derived from information supplied to the computer in the ordinary course of those activities.

(3)   Where over a period the function of storing or processing information for the purposes of any activities regularly carried on over that period as mentioned in subsection (2)(a) above was regularly performed by computers, whether

(a)   by a combination of computers operating over that period; or

(b)   by different computers operating in succession over that period; or

(c)   by different combinations of computers operating in succession over that period; or

(d)   in any other manner involving the successive operation over that period, in whatever order, of one or more computers and one or more combinations of computers,

all the computers used for that purpose during that period shall be treated for the purposes of this Part of this Act as constituting a single computer; and references in this Part of this Act to a computer shall be construed accordingly.

(4)   In any civil proceedings where it is desired to give a statement in evidence by virtue of this section, a certificate doing any of the following things, that is to say:

(a)   identifying the document containing the statement and describing the manner in which it was produced;

(b)   giving such particulars of any device involved in the production of that document as may be appropriate for the purpose of showing that the document was produced by a computer;

(c)   dealing with any of the matters to which the conditions mentioned in subsection (2) above relate,

and purporting to be signed by a person occupying a responsible position in relation to the operation of the relevant device or the management of the relevant activities (whichever is appropriate) shall be evidence of any matter stated in the certificate; and for the purposes of this sub-section it shall be sufficient for a matter to be stated to the best of the knowledge and belief of the person stating it.

(5)　For the purposes of this Part of this Act.

    (a)　information shall be taken to be supplied to a computer if it is supplied thereto in any appropriate form and whether it is so supplied directly or (with or without human intervention) by means of any appropriate equipment;

    (b)　where, in the course of activities carried on by any individual or body, information is supplied with a view to its being stored or processed for the purposes of those activities by a computer operated otherwise than in the course of those activities, that information, if duly supplied to that computer, shall be taken to be supplied to it in the course of those activities;

    (c)　a document shall be taken to have been produced by a computer whether it was produced by it directly or (with or without human intervention) by means of any appropriate equipment.

(6)　Subject to subsection (3) above, in this Part of this Act 'computer' means any device for storing and processing information, and any reference to information being derived from other information is a reference to its being derived therefrom by calculation, comparison or any other process.

Provisions supplementary to ss. 2 to 5.

6.　(1)　Where in any civil proceedings a statement contained in a document is proposed to be given in evidence by virtue of section 2, 4 or 5 of this Act it may, subject to any rules of court, be proved by the production of that document or (whether or not that document is still in existence) by the production of a copy of that document, or of the material part thereof, authenticated in such manner as the court may approve.

(2)　For the purpose of deciding whether or not a statement is admissible in evidence by virtue of section 2, 4 or 5 of this Act the court may draw any reasonable inference from the circumstances in which the statement was made or otherwise came into being or from any other circumstances, including, in the case of a statement contained in a document, the form and contents of that document.

(3)   In estimating the weight, if any, to be attached to a statement admissible in evidence by virtue of section 2, 3, 4 or 5 of this Act regard shall be had to all the circumstances from which any inference can reasonably be drawn as to the accuracy or otherwise of the statement and, in particular

(a)   in the case of a statement falling within section 2(1) or 3(1) or (2) of this Act, to the question whether or not the statement was made contemporaneously with the occurrence or existence of the facts stated, and to the question whether or not the maker of the statement had any incentive to conceal or misrepresent the facts;

(b)   in the case of a statement falling within section 4(1) of this Act, to the question whether or not the person who originally supplied the information from which the record containing the statement was compiled did so contemporaneously with the occurrence or existence of the facts dealt with in that information, and to the question whether or not that person, or any person concerned with compiling or keeping the record containing the statement, had any incentive to conceal or misrepresent the facts; and

(c)   in the case of a statement falling within section 5(1) of this Act, to the question whether or not the information which the information contained in the statement reproduces or is derived from was supplied to the relevant computer, or recorded for the purpose of being supplied thereto, contemporaneously with the occurrence or existence of the facts dealt with in that information, and to the question whether or not any person concerned with the supply of information to that computer, or with the operation of that computer or any equipment by means of which the document containing the statement was produced by it, had any incentive to conceal or misrepresent the facts.

(4)   For the purpose of any enactment or rule of law or practice

requiring evidence to be corroborated or regulating the manner in which uncorroborated evidence is to be treated

(a) a statement which is admissible in evidence by virtue of section 2 or 3 of this Act shall not be capable of corroborating evidence given by the maker of the statement; and

(b) a statement which is admissible in evidence by virtue of section 4 of this Act shall not be capable of corroborating evidence given by the person who originally supplied the information from which the record containing the statement was compiled.

(5) If any person in a certificate tendered in evidence in civil proceedings by virtue of section 5(4) of this Act wilfully makes a statement material in those proceedings which he knows to be false or does not believe to be true, he shall be liable on conviction on indictment to imprisonment for a term not exceeding two years or a fine or both.

Admissibility of evidence as to credibility of maker etc. of statement admitted under s. 2 or 4.

7. (1) Subject to rules of court, where in any civil proceedings a statement made by a person who is not called as a witness in those proceedings is given in evidence by virtue of section 2 of this Act:

(a) any evidence which, if that person had been so called, would be admissible for the purpose of destroying or supporting his credibility as a witness shall be admissible for that purpose in those proceedings; and

(b) evidence tending to prove that, whether before or after he made that statement, that person made (whether orally or in a document or otherwise) another statement inconsistent therewith shall be admissible for the purpose of showing that that person has contradicted himself:

Provided that nothing in this subsection shall enable evidence to be given of any matter of which, if the person in question had been called as a witness and had denied that matter in cross-examination, evidence could not have been adduced by the cross-examining party.

(2)   Subsection (1) above shall apply in relation to a statement given in evidence by virtue of section 4 of this Act as it applies in relation to a statement given in evidence by virtue of section 2 of this Act, except that references to the person who made the statement and to his making the statement shall be construed respectively as references to the person who originally supplied the information from which the record containing the statement was compiled and to his supplying that information.

(3)   Section 3(1) of this Act shall apply to any statement proved by virtue of subsection (1)(b) above as it applies to a previous inconsistent or contradictory statement made by a person called as a witness which is proved as mentioned in paragraph (a) of the said section 3(1).

Rules of court

8.   (1)   Provision shall be made by rules of court as to the procedure which, subject to any exceptions provided for in the rules, must be followed and the other conditions which, subject as aforesaid, must be fulfilled before a statement can be given in evidence in civil proceedings by virtue of section 2, 4 or 5 of this Act.

(2)   Rules of court made in pursuance of subsection (1) above shall in particular, subject to such exceptions (if any) as may be provided for in the rules

(a)   require a party to any civil proceedings who desires to give in evidence any such statement as is mentioned in that subsection to give to every other party to the proceedings such notice of his desire to do so and such particulars of or relating to the statement as may be specified in the rules, including particulars of such one or more of the persons connected with the making or recording of the statement or, in the case of a statement falling within section 5(1) of this Act, such one or more of the persons concerned as mentioned in section 6(3)(c) of this Act as the rules may in any case require; and

(b)   enable any party who receives such notice as aforesaid by counter-notice to require any person of whom particulars were given with the notice to be called as a witness in the proceedings unless that person is dead, or beyond the seas, or unfit by reason of his bodily or mental condition to attend as a witness, or cannot with reasonable diligence be identified or found, or cannot reasonably be expected (having regard to the time which has elapsed since he was connected or concerned as aforesaid and to all the circumstances) to have any recollection of matters relevant to the accuracy or otherwise of the statement.

(3) Rules of the court made in pursuance of subsection (1) above

   (a) may confer on the court in any civil proceedings a discretion to allow a statement falling within section 2(1), 4(1) or 5(1) of this Act to be given in evidence notwithstanding that any requirement of the rules affecting the admissibility of that statement has not been complied with, but except in pursuance of paragraph (b) below shall not confer on the court a discretion to exclude such a statement where the requirements of the rules affecting its admissibility have been complied with;

   (b) may confer on the court power, where a party to any civil proceedings has given notice that he desires to give in evidence

      (i) a statement falling within section 2(1) of this Act which was made by a person, whether orally or in a document, in the course of giving evidence in some other legal proceedings (whether civil or criminal); or

      (ii) a statement falling within section 4(1) of this Act which is contained in a record of any direct oral evidence given in some other legal proceedings (whether civil or criminal),

to give directions on the application of any party to the proceedings as to whether, and if so on what conditions, the party desiring to give the statement in evidence will be permitted to do so and (where applicable) as to the manner in which that statement and any other evidence given in those other proceedings is to be proved; and

(c)   may make different provision for different circumstances, and in particular may make different provision with respect to statements falling within sections 2(1), 4(1) and 5(1) of this Act respectively;

and any discretion conferred on the court by rules of court made as aforesaid may be either a general discretion or a discretion exercisable only in such circumstances as may be specified in the rules.

(4)   Rules of court may make provision for preventing a party to any civil proceedings (subject to any exceptions provided for in the rules) from adducing in relation to a person who is not called as a witness in those proceedings any evidence which could otherwise be adduced by him by virtue of section 7 of this Act unless that party has in pursuance of the rules given in respect of that person such a counter-notice as is mentioned in subsection (2)(b) above.

(5)   In deciding for the purposes of any rules of court made in pursuance of this section whether or not a person is fit to attend as a witness, a court may act on a certificate purporting to be a certificate of a fully registered medical practitioner.

(6)   Nothing in the foregoing provisions of this section shall prejudice the generality of section 99 of the Supreme Court of Judicature (Consolidation) Act 1925, section 102 of the County Courts Act 1959, section 15 of the Justices of the Peace Act 1949 or any other enactment conferring power to make rules of court; and nothing in section 101 of the Supreme Court of Judicature (Consolidation) Act 1925, section 102(2) of the County Courts Act 1959 or any other enactment restricting the matters with respect to which rules of court may be made shall prejudice the making of rules of court with respect to any matter mentioned in the foregoing provisions of this section or the operation of any rules of court made with respect to any such matter.

Admissibility of certain hearsay evidence formerly admissible at common law.

9. (1) In any civil proceedings a statement which, if this Part of this Act had not been passed, would by virtue of any rule of law mentioned in subsection (2) below have been admissible as evidence of any fact stated therein shall be admissible as evidence of that fact by virtue of this subsection.

    (2) The rules of law referred to in subsection (1) above are the following, that is to say any rule of law
- (a) whereby in any civil proceedings an admission adverse to a party to the proceedings, whether made by that party or by another person, may be given in evidence against that party for the purpose of proving any fact stated in the admission;
- (b) whereby in any civil proceedings published works dealing with matters of a public nature (for example, histories, scientific works, dictionaries and maps) are admissible as evidence of facts of a public nature stated therein;
- (c) whereby in any civil proceedings public documents (for example, public registers, and returns made under public authority with respect to matters of public interest) are admissible as evidence of facts stated therein; or
- (d) whereby in any civil proceedings records (for example, the records of certain courts, treaties, Crown grants, pardons and commissions) are admissible as evidence of facts stated therein.

      In this subsection 'admission' includes any representation of fact, whether made in words or otherwise.

    (3) In any civil proceedings a statement which tends to establish reputation or family tradition with respect to any matter and which, if this Act had not been passed, would have been admissible in evidence by virtue of any rule of law mentioned in subsection (4) below.
- (a) shall be admissible in evidence by virtue of this paragraph in so far as it is not capable of being rendered admissible under section 2 or 4 of this Act; and

(b) if given in evidence under this Part of this Act (whether by virtue of paragraph (a) above or otherwise) shall by virtue of this paragraph be admissible as evidence of the matter reputed or handed down;

and, without prejudice to paragraph (b) above, reputation shall for the purposes of this Part of this Act be treated as a fact and not as a statement or multiplicity of statements dealing with the matter reputed.

(4) The rules of law referred to in subsection (3) above are the following, that is to say any rule of law
(a) whereby in any civil proceedings evidence of a person's reputation is admissible for the purpose of establishing his good or bad character;
(b) whereby in any civil proceedings involving a question of pedigree or in which the existence of a marriage is in issue evidence of reputation or family tradition is admissible for the purpose of proving or disproving pedigree or the existence of the marriage, as the case may be; or
(c) whereby in any civil proceedings evidence of reputation or family tradition is admissible for the purpose of proving or disproving the existence of any public or general right or of identifying any person or thing.

(5) It is hereby declared that in so far as any statement is admissible in any civil proceedings by virtue of subsection (1) or (3)(a) above, it may be given in evidence in those proceedings notwithstanding anything in sections 2 to 7 of this Act or in any rules of court made in pursuance of section 8 of this Act.

(6) The words in which any rule of law mentioned in subsection (2) or (4) above is there described are intended only to identify the rule in question and shall not be construed as altering that rule in any way.

Interpretation of Part I, and application to arbitrations, etc.
10. (1) In this Part of this Act
'computer' has the meaning assigned by section 5 of this Act;
'document' includes, in addition to a document in writing:

99

(a) any map, plan, graph or drawing;

(b) any photograph;

(c) any disc, tape, sound track or other device in which sounds or other data (not being visual images) are embodied so as to be capable (with or without the aid of some other equipment) of being reproduced therefrom; and

(d) any film, negative, tape or other device in which one or more visual images are embodied so as to be capable (as aforesaid) of being reproduced therefrom;

'film' includes a microfilm;

'statement' includes any representation of fact, whether made in words or otherwise.

(2) In this Part of this Act any reference to a copy of a document includes

(a) in the case of a document falling within paragraph (c) but not (d) of the definition of 'document' in the foregoing subsection, a transcript of the sounds or other data embodied therein;

(b) in the case of a document falling within paragraph (d) but not (c) of that definition, a reproduction or still reproduction of the image or images embodied therein, whether enlarged or not;

(c) in the case of a document falling within both those paragraphs, such a transcript together with such a still reproduction; and

(d) in the case of a document not falling within the said paragraph (d) of which a visual image is embodied in a document falling within that paragraph, a reproduction of that image, whether enlarged or not,

and any reference to a copy of the material part of a document shall be construed accordingly.

(3) For the purposes of the application of this Part of this Act in relation to any such civil proceedings as are mentioned in section 18(1)(a) and (b) of this Act, any rules of court made for the purposes of this Act under section 99 of the Supreme Court of Judicature (Consolidation) Act 1925 shall (except in so far as their operation is excluded by agreement) apply, subject to such modifications as may be appropriate, in like

manner as they apply in relation to civil proceedings in the High Court:

Provided that in the case of a reference under section 92 of the County Courts Act 1959 this subsection shall have effect as if for the references to the said section 99 and to civil proceedings in the High Court there were substituted respectively references to section 102 of the County Courts Act 1959 and to proceedings in a county court.

(4)   If any question arises as to what are, for the purposes of any such civil proceedings as are mentioned in section 18(1)(a) or (b) of this Act, the appropriate modifications of any such rule of court as is mentioned in subsection (3) above, that question shall, in default of agreement, be determined by the tribunal or the arbitrator or umpire, as the case may be.

(Sections 11–17 inclusive and the schedule have been omitted as being beyond the scope of this book)

Part II

General interpretation, and savings.
18.   (1)   In this Act 'civil proceedings' includes, in addition to civil proceedings in any of the ordinary courts of law –
    (a)   civil proceedings before any other tribunal, being proceedings in relation to which the strict rules of evidence apply; and
    (b)   an arbitration or reference, whether under an enactment or not,
but does not include civil proceedings in relation to which the strict rules of evidence do not apply.

(2)   In this Act
'court' does not include a court-martial, and, in relation to an arbitration or reference, means the arbitrator or umpire and, in relation to proceedings before a tribunal (not being one of the ordinary courts of law), means the tribunal:
'legal proceedings' includes an arbitration or reference, whether under an enactment or not;
and for the avoidance of doubt it is hereby declared that in

this Act, and in any amendment made by this Act in any other enactment, references to a person's husband or wife do not include references to a person who is no longer married to that person.

(3) Any reference in this Act to any other enactment is a reference thereto as amended, and includes a reference thereto as applied, by or under any other enactment.

(4) Nothing in this Act shall prejudice the operation of any enactment which provides (in whatever words) that any answer or evidence given by a person in specified circumstances shall be admissible in evidence against him or some other person in any proceedings or class of proceedings (however described).

In this subsection the reference to giving evidence is a reference to giving evidence in any manner, whether by furnishing information, making discovery, producing documents or otherwise.

(5) Nothing in this Act shall prejudice
   (a) any power of a court, in any legal proceedings, to exclude evidence (whether by preventing questions from being put or otherwise) at its discretion; or
   (b) the operation of any agreement (whenever made) between the parties to any legal proceedings as to the evidence which is to be admissible (whether generally or for any particular purpose) in those proceedings.

(6) It is hereby declared that where, by reason of any defect of speech or hearing from which he is suffering, a person called as a witness in any legal proceedings gives his evidence in writing or by signs, that evidence is to be treated for the purposes of this Act as being given orally.

Short title, repeals, extent and commencement.
20. (1) This Act may be cited as the Civil Evidence Act 1968.

(2) Sections 1, 2, 6(1) (except the words from 'Proceedings' to 'references') and 6(2)(b) of the Evidence Act 1938 are hereby repealed.

(3) This Act shall not extend to Scotland or to Northern Ireland.

(4)   The following provisions of this Act, namely sections 13 to 19, this section (except subsection (2)) and the Schedule, shall come into force on the day this Act is passed, and the other provisions of this Act shall come into force on such day as the Lord Chancellor may by order made by statutory instrument appoint; and different days may be so appointed for different purposes of this Act or for the same purposes in relation to different courts or proceedings or otherwise in relation to different circumstances.

CIVIL EVIDENCE ACT 1972

Application of Part I of Civil Evidence Act 1968 to statements of opinion.

1.   (1)   Subject to the provisions of this section, Part I (hearsay evidence) of the Civil Evidence Act 1968, except section 5 (statements produced by computers), shall apply in relation to statements of opinion as it applies in relation to statements of fact, subject to the necessary modifications and in particular the modification that any reference to a fact stated in a statement shall be construed as a reference to a matter dealt with therein.

     (2)   Section 4 (admissibility of certain records) of the Civil Evidence Act 1968, as applied by subsection (1) above, shall not render admissible in any civil proceedings a statement of opinion contained in a record unless that statement would be admissible in those proceedings if made in the course of giving oral evidence by the person who originally supplied the information from which the record was compiled; but where a statement of opinion contained in a record deals with a matter on which the person who originally supplied the information from which the record was compiled is (or would if living be) qualified to give oral expert evidence, the said section 4, as applied by subsection (I) above, shall have effect in relation to that statement as if so much of subsection (1) of that section as requires personal knowledge on the part of that person were omitted.

Rules of court with respect to expert reports and oral expert evidence.
2. (1)   If and so far as rules of court so provide, sub-section (2) of section 2 of the Civil Evidence Act 1968 (which imposes restrictions on the giving of a statement in evidence by virtue of that section on behalf of a party who has called or intends to call as a witness the maker of the statement) shall not apply to statements (whether of fact or opinion) contained in expert reports.

   (2)   In so far as they relate to statements (whether of fact or opinion) contained in expert reports, rules of court made in pursuance of subsection (1) of section 8 of the Civil Evidence Act 1968 as to the procedure to be followed and the other conditions to be fulfilled before a statement can be given in evidence in civil proceedings by virtue of section 2 of that Act (admissibility of out-of-court statements) shall not be subject to the requirements of subsection (2) of the said section 8 (which specifies certain matters of procedure for which provision must ordinarily be made by rules of court made in pursuance of the said subsection (1)).

   (3)   Notwithstanding any enactment or rule of law by virtue of which documents prepared for the purpose of pending or contemplated civil proceedings or in connection with the obtaining or giving of legal advice are in certain circumstances privileged from disclosure, provision may be made by rules of court
      (a)   for enabling the court in any civil proceedings to direct, with respect to medical matters or matters of any other class which may be specified in the direction, that the parties or some of them shall each by such date as may be so specified (or such later date as may be permitted or agreed in accordance with the rules) disclose to the other or others in the form of one or more expert reports the expert evidence on matters of that class which he proposes to adduce as part of his case at the trial; and
      (b)   for prohibiting a party who fails to comply with a direction given in any such proceedings under rules of

court made by virtue of paragraph (a) above from adducing in evidence by virtue of section 2 of the Civil Evidence Act 1968 (admissibility of out-of-court statements), except with the leave of the court, any statement (whether of fact or opinion) contained in any expert report whatsoever in so far as that statement deals with matters of any class specified in the direction.

(4) Provision may be made by rules of court as to the conditions subject to which oral expert evidence may be given in civil proceedings.

(5) Without prejudice to the generality of subsection (4) above, rules of court made in pursuance of that subsection may make provision for prohibiting a party who fails to comply with a direction given as mentioned in subsection (3)(b) above from adducing, except with the leave of the court, any oral expert evidence whatsoever with respect to matters of any class specified in the direction.

(6) Any rules of court made in pursuance of this section may make different provision for different classes of cases, for expert reports dealing with matters of different classes, and for other different circumstances.

(7) References in this section to an expert report are references to a written report by a person dealing wholly or mainly with matters on which he is (or would if living be) qualified to give expert evidence.

(8) Nothing in the foregoing provisions of this section shall prejudice the generality of section 99 of the Supreme Court of Judicature (Consolidation) Act 1925, section 102 of the County Courts Act 1959, section 15 of the Justices of the Peace Act 1949 or any other enactment conferring power to make rules of court; and nothing in section 101 of the said Act of 1925, section 102(2) of the County Courts Act 1959 or any other enactment restricting the matters with respect to which rules of court may be made shall prejudice the making of rules of court in pursuance of this section or the operation of any rules of court so made.

Admissibility of expert opinion and certain expressions of non-expert opinion.

3. (1) Subject to any rules of court made in pursuance of Part I of the Civil Evidence Act 1968 or this Act, where a person is called as a witness in any civil proceedings, his opinion on any relevant matter on which he is qualified to give expert evidence shall be admissible in evidence.

    (2) It is hereby declared that where a person is called as a witness in any civil proceedings, a statement of opinion by him on any relevant matter on which he is not qualified to give expert evidence, if made as a way of conveying relevant facts personally perceived by him, is admissible as evidence of what he perceived.

    (3) In this section 'relevant matter' includes an issue in the proceedings in question.

Evidence of foreign law.

4. (1) It is hereby declared that in civil proceedings a person who is suitably qualified to do so on account of his knowledge or experience is competent to give expert evidence as to the law of any country or territory outside the United Kingdom, or of any part of the United Kingdom other than England and Wales, irrespective of whether he has acted or is entitled to act as a legal practitioner there.

    (2) Where any question as to the law of any country or territory outside the United Kingdom, or of any part of the United Kingdom other than England and Wales, with respect to any matter has been determined (whether before or after the passing of this Act) in any such proceedings as are mentioned in subsection (4) below, then in any civil proceedings (not being proceedings before a court which can take judicial notice of the law of that country, territory or part with respect to that matter).

    (a) any finding made or decision given on that question in the first-mentioned proceedings shall, if reported or recorded in citable form, be admissible in evidence for the purpose of proving the law of that country, territory or part with respect to that matter; and

(b) if that finding or decision, as so reported or recorded, is adduced for that purpose, the law of the country, territory or part with respect to that matter shall be taken to be in accordance with that finding or decision unless the contrary is proved:

Provided that paragraph (b) above shall not apply in the case of a finding or decision which conflicts with another finding or decision on the same question adduced by virtue of this subsection in the same proceedings.

(3) Except with the leave of the court, a party to any civil proceedings shall not be permitted to adduce any such finding or decision as is mentioned in subsection (2) above by virtue of that subsection unless he has in accordance with rules of court given to every other party to the proceedings notice that he intends to do so.

(4) The proceedings referred to in subsection (2) above are the following, whether civil or criminal, namely
   (a) proceedings at first instance in any of the following courts, namely the High Court, the Crown Court, a court of quarter sessions, the Court of Chancery of the county palatine of Lancaster and the Court of Chancery of the county palatine of Durham;
   (b) appeals arising out of any such proceedings as are mentioned in paragraph (a);
   (c) proceedings before the Judicial Committee of the Privy Council on appeal (whether to Her Majesty in Council or to the Judicial Committee as such) from any decision of any court outside the United Kingdom.

(5) For the purposes of this section a finding or decision on any such question as is mentioned in subsection (2) above shall be taken to be reported or recorded in citable form if, but only if, it is reported or recorded in writing in a report, transcript or other document which, if that question had been a question as to the law of England and Wales, could be cited as an authority in legal proceedings in England and Wales.

Interpretation, application to arbitrations etc. and savings.

5.   (1) In this Act 'civil proceedings' and 'court' have the meanings assigned by section 18(1) and (2) of the Civil Evidence Act 1968.

    (2) Subsections (3) and (4) of section 10 of the Civil Evidence Act 1968 shall apply for the purposes of the application of sections 2 and 4 of this Act in relation to any such civil proceedings as are mentioned in section 18(1)(a) and (b) of that Act (that is to say civil proceedings before a tribunal other than one of the ordinary courts of law, being proceedings in relation to which the strict rules of evidence apply, and an arbitration or reference, whether under an enactment or not) as they apply for the purposes of the application of Part I of that Act in relation to any such civil proceedings.

    (3) Nothing in this Act shall prejudice
      (a) any power of a court, in any civil proceedings, to exclude evidence (whether by preventing questions from being put or otherwise) as its direction; or
      (b) the operation of any agreement (whenever made) between the parties to any civil proceedings as to the evidence which is to be admissible (whether generally or for any particular purpose) in those proceedings.

Short title, extent and commencement.

6.   (1) This Act may be cited at the Civil Evidence Act 1972.

    (2) This Act shall not extend to Scotland or Northern Ireland.

    (3) This Act, except sections 1 and 4(2) to (5), shall come into force on 1st January 1973, and sections 1 and 4(2) to (5) shall come into force on day as the Lord Chancellor may by order made by statutory instrument appoint; and different days may be so appointed for different purposes or for the same purposes in relation to different courts or proceedings or otherwise in relation to different circumstances.

EXTRACTS FROM THE RULES OF THE SUPREME COURT

Order 38

Evidence: General rules

Rule 1   General rule: witnesses to be examined orally
Subject to the provisions of these rules and of the Civil Evidence Act 1968, and any other enactment relating to evidence, any fact required to be proved at the trial of any action begun by writ by the evidence of witnesses shall be proved by the examination of the witnesses orally and in open court.

Examination of witnesses –

Examination-in-chief. – In examination-in-chief leading questions may not as a rule be put, but the Court has a discretion to relax the rule so far as justice may require. A witness may refresh his memory by referring to any writing made by himself at the time of the transaction about which he is being examined, or at any subsequent time if the Court considers it was then fresh in his memory, or even if made by another person if read within such time by the witness, and if when he read it he knew it to be correct. And an expert witness may refresh his memory by reference to professional treatises. But any such writing or treatise must be shown to the adverse party if he requires it, and he may cross-examine upon it. The evidence in chief must be confined to facts within the witness's own knowledge, except where he is called as an expert on questions on which expert evidence is admissible, *e.g.*, handwriting, science, or trade.
Cross-examination. – In cross-examination leading questions may in general be put, and the right to cross-examine is not limited by the examination-in-chief but extends to the whole case.
Re-examination. – There is a right to re-examine to explain answers given in cross-examination.
Exclusion of witnesses from the Court – On the application of either party the Court may at any time order all witnesses on both sides, other than the one under examination, to withdraw, but not to leave the Court again after giving evidence so as to communicate with other witnesses before they give evidence.

Rule 2   Evidence by affidavit
(1)   The Court may, at or before the trial of an action begun by writ, order that the affidavit of any witness may be read at the trial if in the circumstances of the case it thinks it reasonable so to order.
(2)   An order under paragraph (1) may be made on such terms as to the filing and giving of copies of the affidavits and as to the production of the deponents for cross-examination as the Court thinks fit but, subject to any such terms and to any subsequent order of the Court, the deponents shall not be subject to cross-examination and need not attend the trial for the purpose.
(3)   In any cause or matter begun by originating summons, originating motion or petition, and on any application made by summons or motion, evidence may be given by affidavit unless in the case of any such cause, matter or application any provision of these rules otherwise provides or the Court otherwise directs, but the Court may, on the application of any party order the attendance for cross-examination of the person making any such affidavit, and where, after such an order has been made, the person in question does not attend, his affidavit shall not be used as evidence without the leave of the Court.

Rule 3   Evidence of particular facts
(1)   Without prejudice to rule 2, the Court may, at or before the trial of any action, order that evidence of any particular fact shall be given at the trial in such manner as may be specified by the order.
(2)   The power conferred by paragraph (1) extends in particular to ordering that evidence of any particular fact may be given at the trial –
   (a)   by statement on oath of information or belief, or
   (b)   by the production of documents or entries in books, or
   (c)   by copies of documents or entries in books, or
   (d)   in the case of a fact which is or was a matter of common knowledge either generally or in a particular district, by the production of a specified newspaper which contains a statement of that fact.

Rule 4   Limitation of expert evidence
The Court may, at or before the trial of any action, order that the number of medical or other expert witnesses who may be called at the trial shall be limited as specified by the order.

Expert witnesses – Their function is (*inter alia*) to explain words, or terms of science or art appearing on the documents which have to be construed by the Court, to give expert assistance to the Court (*e.g.,* as to the laws of science, or the working of a technical process or system) or to inform the court as to the state of public knowledge with regard to the matters before it.

Rule 5   *Limitation of plans, etc. in evidence*
Unless, at or before the trial, the Court for special reasons otherwise orders, no plan, photograph or model shall be receivable in evidence at the trial of an action unless at least 10 days before the commencement of the trial the parties, other than the party producing it, have been given an opportunity to inspect it and to agree to the admission thereof without further proof.

Rule 6   *Revocation or variation of orders under rules 2 to 5*
Any order under rules 2 to 5 (including an order made on appeal) may, on sufficient cause being shown, be revoked or varied by a subsequent order of the Court made at or before the trial.

Rule 36   *Restrictions on adducing expert evidence*
(1)   Except with the leave of the Court or where all parties agree, no expert evidence may be adduced at the trial or hearing of any cause or matter unless the party seeking to adduce the evidence (a) has applied to the Court to determine whether a direction should be given under rule 3, 38 or 41 (whichever is appropriate) and has complied with any direction given on the application or (b) has complied with automatic directions taking effect under Order 25 rule 8 (1)(b).

(2)   Nothing in paragraph (1) shall apply to evidence which is permitted to be given by affidavit or shall affect the enforcement under any other provision of these Rules (except Order 45, rule 5) of a direction given under this Part of this Order.

Rule 37   *Expert evidence in actions for personal injuries*
(1)   This rule applies to any action for personal injuries, except –
    (a)   any Admiralty action; and
    (b)   any action where the pleadings contain an allegation of a negligent act or omission in the course of medical treatment.

(2)   Where an application is made under rule 36(1) in respect of oral expert evidence, then, unless the Court considers that there is

sufficient reason for not doing so, it shall direct that the substance of the evidence be disclosed in the form of a written report or reports to such other parties and within such period as the Court may specify.

(3) Where the expert evidence relates to medical matters the Court may, if it thinks fit, treat the following circumstances as sufficient reason for not giving a direction under paragraph (2), namely that the expert evidence may contain an expression of opinion —
  (i) as to the manner in which the personal injuries were sustained; or
  (ii) as to the genuineness of the symptoms of which complaint is made.

(4) Where the expert evidence does not relate to medical matters, the Court may, if it thinks fit, treat as a sufficient reason for not giving a direction under paragraph (2) any of the circumstances set out in sub-paragraphs (a) or (b) of rule 38(2).

Rule 38   Expert evidence in other actions

(1) Where an application is made under rule 36(1) in respect of oral expert evidence to which rule 37 does not apply, the Court may, if satisfied that it is desirable to do so, direct that the substance of any expert evidence which is to be adduced by any party be disclosed in the form of a written report or reports to such other parties and within such period as the Court may specify.

(2) In deciding whether to give a direction under paragraph (1) the Court shall have regard to all the circumstances and may, to such extent as it thinks fit, treat any of the following circumstances as affording a sufficient reason for not giving such a direction:-
  (a) that the expert evidence is or will be based to any material extent upon a verson of the facts in dispute between he parties; or
  (b) that the expert evidence is or will be based to any material extent upon facts which are neither —
    (i) ascertainable by the expert by the exercise of his own powers of observation, nor
    (ii) within his general professional knowledge and experience.

Rule 39   Disclosure of part of expert evidence

Where the Court considers that any circumstances rendering it undesirable to give a direction under rule 37 or 38 relate to part only of the evidence sought to be adduced, the Court may, if it thinks fit, direct disclosure of the remainder.

Rule 41   Expert evidence contained in statement
Where an application is made under rule 36 in respect of expert evidence in a statement and the applicant alleges that the maker of the statement cannot or should not be called as a witness, the Court may direct that the provisions of rules 20 to 23 and 25 to 33 shall apply with such modifications as the Court thinks fit.

Rule 42   Putting in evidence expert report disclosed by another party
A party to any cause or matter may put in evidence any expert report disclosed to him by any other party in accordance with this part of this Order.

Rule 43   Time for putting expert report in evidence
Where a party to any cause or matter calls as a witness the maker of a report which has been disclosed in accordance with rule 40 or in accordance with a direction given under rule 37 or 38, the report may be put in evidence at the commencement of its maker's examination in chief or at such other time as the Court may direct.

Rule 44   Revocation and variation of directions
Any direction given under this Part of this Order may on sufficient cause being shown be revoked or varied by a subsequent direction given at or before the trial of the cause or matter.

Order 40

Court Expert

Rule 1   Appointment of expert to report on certain questions
(1)   In any cause or matter which is to be tried without a jury and in which any question for an expert witness arises the Court may at any time, on the application of any party, appoint an independent expert or, if more than one such question arises, two or more such experts, to inquire and report upon any question of fact or opinion not involving questions of law or of constructon.

An expert appointed under this paragraph is referred to in this Order as a 'court expert.'

(2) Any court expert in a cause or matter shall, if possible, be a person agreed between the parties and, failing agreement, shall be nominated by the Court.

(3) The question to be submitted to the court expert and the instructions (if any) given to him shall, failing agreement between the parties, be settled by the Court.

(4) In this rule 'expert,' in relation to any question arising in a cause or matter, means any person who has such knowledge or experience of or in connection with that question that his opinion on it would be admissible in evidence.

Rule 2 *Report of court expert*

(1) The court expert must send his report to the Court, together with such number of copies thereof as the Court may direct, and the proper officer must send copies of the report to the parties or their solicitors.

(2) The Court may direct the court expert to make a further or supplemental report.

(3) Any part of a court expert's report which is not accepted by all the parties to the cause or matter in which it is made shall be treated as information furnished to the Court and be given such weight as the Court thinks fit.

Rule 3 *Experiments and tests*

If the court expert is of opinion that an experiment or test of any kind (other than one of a trifling character) is necessary to enable him to make a satisfactory report he shall inform the parties or their solicitors and shall, if possible, make an arrangement with them as to the expenses involved, the persons to attend and other relevant matters; and if the parties are unable to agree on any of those matters it shall be settled by the Court.

Rule 4 *Cross-examination of court expert*

Any party may, within 14 days after receiving a copy of the court expert's report, apply to the Court for leave to cross-examine the expert on his report, and on that application the Court shall make an order for the cross-examination of the expert by all the parties either

    (a)   at the trial, or

(b) before an examiner at such time and place as may be specified in the order.

Rule 5   Remuneration of court expert
(1) The remuneration of the court expert shall be fixed by the Court and shall include a fee for his report and a proper sum for each day during which he is required to be present either in court or before an examiner.
(2) Without prejudice to any order providing for payment of the court expert's remuneration as part of the costs of the cause or matter, the parties shall be jointly and severally liable to pay the amount fixed by the Court for his remuneration, but where the appointment of a court expert is opposed the Court may, as a condition of making the appointment, require the party applying for the appointment to give such security for the remuneration of the expert as the Court thinks fit.

Rule 6   Calling of expert witnesses
Where a court expert is appointed in a cause or matter, any party may, on giving to the other parties a reasonable time before the trial notice of his intention to do so, call one expert witness to give evidence on the question reported on by the court expert but no party may call more than one such witness without the leave of the Court, and the Court shall not grant leave unless it considers the circumstances of the case to be exceptional.

EXTRACTS FROM THE LANDS TRIBUNAL RULES

Sittings of Tribunal
(1) The Tribunal shall sit at such places in England and Wales as the President may from time to time determine.
(2) The registrar shall send to each party to proceedings before the Tribunal a notice informing him of the place and date of the hearing which, unless the parties otherwise agree, shall not be earlier than 14 days after the date on which the notice is sent.
(3) Upon receiving notice of intention to appear from a person who is not already a party to the proceedings, the registrar shall send to that person a notice informing him of the place and date of the hearing.

(4)   Any person to whom notice has been sent under paragraph (2) or
       (3) above may apply to the registrar in accordance with the
       provisions of rule 45 for an alteration of the place or date of the
       hearing.

Tribunal to sit in public
The Tribunal shall sit in public except where it is acting as arbitrator
under a reference by consent.

View of land
(1)   Subject to the provisions of paragraph (2) below, the Tribunal
       may inspect the land or hereditament which is the subject of the
       proceedings and may, if it thinks fit, enter on the land or heredita-
       ment for that purpose.
(2)   When the Tribunal intends to enter on any premises in pursuance
       of paragraph (1) above, it shall give notice to the parties of that
       intention and the parties shall be entitled to attend the inspection.
(3)   The provisions of this rule shall apply, so far as practicable, to any
       comparable land or hereditament to which the attention of the
       Tribunal is directed as they apply to the land or hereditament
       which is the subject of the proceedings.

Assessors
(1)   If it appears to the President that any case coming before the
       Tribunal calls for special knowledge and that it would be desir-
       able for the Tribunal to sit with assessors, he may direct that the
       Tribunal shall hear the case with the aid of an assessor or asses-
       sors appointed by him after any consultations he may think fit.
(2)   The remuneration to be paid to any assessor appointed under this
       rule shall be such as the President may, with the approval of the
       Minister for the Civil Service, determine.

Proceedings to be consolidated or heard together
(1)   Where more than one notice of appeal has been given in respect
       of the same land or hereditament, an application to the registrar
       in accordance with the provisions of rule 45 for an order that the
       appeals be consolidated may be made by any party to the appeals.
(2)   Where two or more notices of appeal have been given in respect
       of different lands or hereditaments raising the same issues or
       where two or more notices of reference have been given in respect

of several interests in the same subject in dispute, an application may be made by any party to the proceedings that the appeals, or as the case may be the references, be heard together.

(3)   Where any such notices of appeal or notices of reference as are referred to in paragraph (1) or (2) above have been given, the President or the Tribunal may, without any application in that behalf, order that the appeals or references be consolidated or heard together.

(4)   An order may be made with respect to some only of the matters to which the notices of appeal or notices of reference relate.

Power to select test case in appeals from local valuation courts
Where two or more appeals against the decision of a local valuation court appear to the President to involve the same issues, he may, with the written consent of all parties to the appeals, direct that one appeal, to be selected by him, shall be heard in the first instance as a test case and that the parties to each appeal shall, without prejudice to their right to require the Tribunal to state a case for the decision of the Court of Appeal, be bound by the decision of the Tribunal on the appeal so selected.

Application of Arbitration Act 1950
Sections 12, 14, 17, 18(5), 20 (subject to any enactment which prescribes a rate of interest) and 26 of the Arbitration Act 1950 shall apply to all proceedings as they apply to an arbitration unless a contrary intention is expressed in the arbitration agreement, and, where the Tribunal is acting as arbitrator under a reference by consent, sections 1, 2, 3, 4(1), 5, 18(3) and (4), 24(2) and (3) and 27 of the Arbitration Act 1950 shall also apply.

Evidence
(1)   Evidence before the Tribunal may be given orally or, if the parties to the proceedings consent or the President or the Tribunal so orders, by affidavit, but the Tribunal may at any stage of the proceedings make an order requiring the personal attendance of any deponent for examination and cross-examination.

(2)   The provisions of paragraphs (2) to (6) of rule 45 shall apply to an application to the President for leave to give evidence by affidavit, with the substitution of references to the President for references to the registrar.

(3)   Nothing in the Civil Evidence Act 1972, or in rules of court made under it, shall prevent expert evidence from being adduced before the Tribunal by any party notwithstanding that no application has been made to the Tribunal for a direction as to the disclosure of that evidence to any other party to the proceedings.

Disclosure of documents

A party to proceedings shall deliver to the registrar on his request any document or other information which the Tribunal may require and which it is in the power of that party to deliver and shall afford to every other party to the proceedings an opportunity to inspect those documents (or copies of them) and to take copies:

Provided that nothing in this rule shall be deemed to require any information to be disclosed contrary to the public interest.

Failure to supply documents

If it appears to the Tribunal that any party to proceedings has failed to send a copy of any document required under these Rules to be sent to any other party or to the registrar, the Tribunal may direct that a copy of the document shall be sent as may be necessary and that the further hearing of the proceedings be adjourned, and may in any such case require the party at fault to pay any additional costs occasioned thereby.

Expert witnesses

(1)   This rule applies to any proceedings except appeals from decisions of local valuation courts under Part II and applications for certificates under Part VI.

(2)   Not more than one expert witness on either side shall be heard unless otherwise ordered:

Provided that, where the proceedings include a claim for compensation in respect of minerals or disturbance of business, as well as in respect of land, one additional expert witness on either side on the value of the minerals or, as the case may be, on the damage suffered by reason of the disturbance may be heard.

(3)   An application for leave to call more than one, or more than one additional, expert witness may be made to the registrar in accordance with the provisions of rule 45 or to the Tribunal at the hearing.

(4) Where more than one party intends to call an expert witness, every such party shall, within 28 days after being so requested by the registrar, send to the registrar a copy of each of the following documents relating to the evidence to be given by the expert witness, together with sufficient copies for service upon the other parties –
   (i) every plan and valuation of the land or hereditament which is the subject of the proceedings (including particulars and computations in support of the valuation) which it is proposed to put in evidence;
   (ii) either a statement of any prices, costs or other particulars and any plans relating to a property or properties other than that land or hereditament which are proposed to be given in evidence in support of the valuation, or a statement that no such prices, costs, particulars or plans will be relied upon.

(5) The registrar shall, within 7 days after receiving all the documents required to be supplied by the parties under paragraph (4) above, send to each party copies of the documents supplied by the other party.

(6) If an application for leave to call more than one, or more than one additional, expert witness is made at the hearing and is granted by the Tribunal, or if at the hearing any party seeks to rely upon any plans, valuations or particulars which appear to the Tribunal not to have been sent to the registrar in accordance with this rule, the Tribunal shall, unless it is satisfied that no prejudice to any other party will arise, adjourn the hearing on such terms as to costs or otherwise as it thinks fit.

EXTRACTS FROM THE LAW REFORM COMMITTEE REPORT

Inferences and Opinions of Experts
7. It frequently occurs, however, in the course of litigation that a judge has to form an opinion upon a matter which calls for some specialised knowledge or experience which he does not possess. It may be something perceptible upon physical examination, but which would be recognised only by someone possessed of special knowledge or experience, such as defects in the quality of goods or physical injuries to a human being. It may be an inference to be

drawn from what has been perceived by witnesses with their physical senses, such as the cause of damage to goods or the diagnosis or prognosis of a disease or physical injury. It may be an opinion as to whether the conduct of a party conforms to a special standard of skill or care that it was his duty in the circumstances to display, as in cases of negligence in a particular profession or trade. In order that the judge may form a correct opinion on matters of these kinds, it is essential that he should be provided with all relevant information about them by someone possessed of the requisite specialised skill and knowledge.

8.   There are various ways in which information of this kind can be provided. One way is by expert assessors sitting with the judge to give him advice which is not generally disclosed (at any rate in detail) to the parties. Another would be to appoint an expert to make a report to the court and to the parties on any matter calling for specialised knowledge or experience. The third, which is the way usually adopted, is for the judge to be supplied with the relevant information by expert witnesses selected and called by the parties and subjected to the usual procedure of examination-in-chief, cross-examination and re-examination.

Expert Evidence adduced by Parties to Civil Proceedings

18.   Expert evidence is admissible upon a matter of kind discussed in paragraph 7, upon which information from persons possessed of special knowledge or experience is needed to enable the judge to form a correct opinion upon an issue in the proceedings. It is for the judge to determine what such matters are, subject to decided cases and settled law, but the test is the general knowledge and experience of judges as a class and not any idiosyncratic specialised knowledge or experience of the individual judge who tries the case. For instance, a judge who was qualified as a doctor could not dispense with expert evidence upon a medical issue because he knew enough about it himself. To do so would be to make it impossible for the parties to avail themselves fully of their right of appeal to a court of appeal, who would not be possessed of similar qualifications and who would require to be instructed by the evidence of experts, of which there would be none.

Qualification of Experts

19. It is also for the judge to determine whether the expert whose testimony is sought to be adduced possesses the knowledge or experience needed to make his evidence of assistance in enabling the judge to form a correct opinion on the matter in issue. But, if the matter is one upon which expert evidence is admissible at all, the qualifications of the expert, if he has any specialised knowledge or experience in the matter, go to the weight of his evidence, not to its admissibility. Parties, in their own interest, will seek to obtain experts with the most impressive qualifications possible and it is, we think, undesirable to lay down as a matter of law any minimum qualification in any class of expertise. It has not in the past been the practice to do so except in one instance, that of experts in foreign law. In the old case of *Bristow* v *Sequeville* (1850) 5 Ex. 275, there are statements which suggest that only a person who has practised, or at least is entitled to practice, in the courts of the foreign state is qualified to give expert evidence about its law. This requirement has been often relaxed in more recent cases. It ought, we think, to be treated as obsolete. Whether a witness to foreign law is a practitioner or not, and the nature of his practice, go to the weight of his evidence, not to its admissibility. A judge is not bound to accept as correct the evidence of expert witnesses on foreign law or any other matter of expertise. If he does not accept it on a matter of foreign law, he must apply the presumption that the relevant foreign law is the same as English law. On other matters of expertise, the effect of his inability to accept as correct the only expert evidence adduced on a particular issue will vary according to where the onus of proof on that issue lies.

Text-books and Writings

20. Experts are entitled, in support of any opinion expressed by them, to refer to a text-book or other written material, whatever its authorship, if it is regarded as authoritative by those qualified in their specialty. Passages which are so referred to become part of the expert's testimony. But, except under these conditions, material contained in text-books or other writings is not admissible unless, of course, the parties so agree. We do not recommend any alteration in this practice. A text-book or other writing

is no more than the opinion of another expert who is not there to explain the application of what he has written to the relevant facts of the case, or to be cross-examined. Of his qualifications and the weight attached to his opinions by those experienced in the same field, the court itself is not in a position to judge without expert assistance.

Oral Evidence of Experts

21. We do not recommend any fundamental change in the method of providing the court with the information necessary to enable the judge to form a correct opinion on matters requiring special knowledge or experience which he does not himself possess. We think that it should continue to be left to the parties to choose and call their own expert witnesses, whose evidence should (except in proceedings where it is the practice to adduce affidavit evidence) be subject to the ordinary process of oral examination, cross-examination and re-examination which is a basic principle of the adversary system. On the other hand, we think that there are a number of procedural changes which would have the two-fold result of reducing controversy on matters of expertise to a minimum and of increasing the usefulness of oral expert evidence on any matters which remain in controversy.

Appendix D

RECOMMENDED FURTHER READING

Guide-lines of good practice for expert witnesses. The Chartered Institute of Arbitrators.

Syllabus for training in the practice and procedure of giving evidence of opinion and expert evidence. The Chartered Institute of Arbitrators.

The Complete Plain Words (Sir Ernest Gowers — revised by Sir Bruce Fraser). HMSO.

The Law Reform Committee Seventeenth Report (Evidence of Opinion and Expert Evidence, October 1970 Cmmd 4489). HMSO.

The Giving of Evidence, The Rt. Hon. Lord Macmillan of Aberfeldy. The Institution of Civil Engineers.

Learning the Law by Glanville Williams. Stevens.
General Principles of English Law (5th Edition) by P. W. D. Redmond. Macdonald & Evans.

Phipsons Manual of the Law of Evidence. Sweet & Maxwell.
English Law (6th Edition) by K. Smith & D. J. Keenan. Pitman.

Table of Cases

Index

Index

129